EduMatch®: Snapshot in Education (2018)

Copyright © 2018 EDUMATCH®
All rights reserved.

EduMatch®:
Snapshot in Education (2018)

Contributing Authors
(by Order of Chapter):

Natasha Rachell | Bonnie Nieves
Elford Rawls-Dill, PhD
Dr. Michael Milstead
William Jeffery
Crystal R. Morgan
David Dutrow | Tyler Witman
Tina Lauer | Desiree Alexander
Susan R. Mosely
Stephanie Filardo
Marvia Davidson | David Lockett
Craig Shapiro | Martine Brown
Rachelle Dene Poth
Sharon H. Porter, Ed.D.
Rian Reed | Jason B. Allen
Amy Storer | Dene E. Gainey

Edited by Sarah Thomas, Ph.D.
Copyright © 2018 EDUMATCH®
All rights reserved.

ACKNOWLEDGMENTS

Thank you to the following chapter editors, who helped to make this book possible:

Martine Brown
Penny Christensen
David Dutrow
Elissa Frazier
Dr. Michael Harvey
Dr. Riina Hirsch
William Jackson
Deborah Kerby
Melody McAllister
Don Sturm
Adina Sullivan-Marlow
Takia Toomer
Nicole Zumpano

DEDICATION

This book is dedicated to the EduMatch® family of educators. Thank you to those of you who have been so willing to share as we continue to learn and grow together.

CONTENTS

USE YOUR WHY TO DRIVE YOUR INTENTION	1
MAKING LESSONS MEMORABLE	19
BETWEEN A ROCK AND A SAFE PLACE	27
PARENT ENGAGEMENT	43
INSTRUCTIONAL COACHING: THE IMPACT OF 360 VIDEO	55
I'VE GOT A FEVER, AND THE ONLY CURE IS MORE FLIPGRID!	65
TEACH ADAPTABILITY, NOT APPS	83
NOVEL ENGINEERING - INTEGRATING STEM AND LITERATURE	89
READY! SET! GO!	111
USING SOCIAL EMOTIONAL LEARNING (SEL) AS THE RUDDER TO NAVIGATE THE WAY	133
CONFESSIONS OF A FIRST YEAR COMPUTER SCIENCE TEACHER	145
THE CREATIVE TEACHER	151
4 C'S OF 21ST CENTURY LEARNING	163
THE 3 PS AND 3 ES	167
THROWING ROCKS INTO THE SOUL	195
POWER OF BEING A CONNECTED EDUCATOR	205
PREPARING TO LEAD: COACHING FOR ASPIRING AND NOVICE SCHOOL LEADERS	237
CULTURALLY COMPETENT TEACHER RECRUITMENT AND RETENTION	253

THE WAR ON BLACK BOYS IN SCHOOLS: BLACK MALE EDUCATORS CAN HELP   **267**
IT ALL BEGAN WITH NANCY   **285**
EVER-CHANGING NATURE & NEEDS   **293**

Use Your Why to Drive Your Intention

Natasha Rachell

When you know your why and live with gratitude, you become more clearly aligned with your purpose and being intentional about what you do each and every day.

Every day you get to make choices. You choose what to wear for the day. You decide what to eat for breakfast, lunch, and dinner. You choose what your attitude will be for the day. You choose how you will interact with your students and colleagues. And you choose the energy that you will bring into your schools and classes each and every day. Are you being intentional as you make these decisions every day?

I don't know about you, but I remember when I first became a teacher. My hiring principal, Ms. Margie Smith, sat me across from her in her office and looked me in the eye. She said to me, "I know you've never been a teacher before, but I see something in you. I'm going to take a chance on you. I'm going to hire you. You're going to make me proud, and you're going to be my star baby." That was back in 2004, and I still remember it like it was yesterday. To this day, as I make decisions as an educator, I strive to make Ms. Smith proud. She is definitely a part of my why.

***

A couple of years ago, my family went through some experiences that totally changed the trajectory of the intention of my life. One of which, and probably the most impactful was my twin brother, Jermaine (image to the left), going through a horrific car accident that left him with a traumatic brain injury. Since this incident, I have seen my life change tenfold because of the

decision to focus on my why and to live with intention. One of my favorite authors is Simon Sinek. He has a few Ted Talks and has written books such as "Leaders

Eat Last" and my personal favorite, "Start with Why." In "Start with Why," Sinek challenges the reader to always focus on the why of what you are doing. He states that once you know your why, the what and the how will come naturally. If you know why you are a teacher, how you teach and what you teach will follow. If you know why you want to pursue a master's or doctoral degree, what you decide to pursue and how you go about completing these goals will come naturally. I challenge you, through reading my experiences, to examine your own why as well as the intention that you will make decisions with each and every day.

During my second year of teaching, I had a group of five males that sat in the back, right-hand corner of my classroom. They were best friends. Whenever you saw 1 of them, you saw the other 4. The first two of them are deceased. One of them was playing Russian roulette during Martin Luther King Day Jr. weekend, shot and killed himself. The other was shot and

Natasha Rachell: Use Your Why to Drive Your Intention

killed a few years ago over a card game in his friend's garage. Two of them are in jail. One was a serial rapist, and the other strangled and killed his girlfriend and her best friend over some money that he claimed they owed him. The fifth one, is Matt (image to the left). Matt is the 1 of 5 that made it. He is a police officer.

He's married. He has a son and he's doing awesome! I speak to Matt about once a month and every time I talk to him, I ask him, "Matt, what was different about your path and your journey? Why did you make different decisions? How did you make it? Without fail, EVERY time I ask him these questions, he ALWAYS responds with, "Mrs. Rachell, I didn't want to let you down." All the feels, right? Now, whether or not Matt is telling me the truth or simply trying to butter me up, I don't know. But what I do know, is that if I had even a small, tiny positive impact on his life, that he wanted to not let me down, I feel 100% honored to have served that part in his life. I don't take that for granted at all.

My Velvet Teddy Bear

I had another student named Sheldon (image to the left). He was my velvet teddy bear! Sheldon was super quiet and did just enough to get by in my class. One day, I gave an assignment to the class as we were studying the water, carbon, and nitrogen cycles. I told them to pick one of the cycles and bring me back a project in a week that showed that they had mastered the standard that we were studying. Sheldon came in the very next day and slammed a CD down on my desk with the words, "Water Cycle Rap" written in black Sharpie marker. He was very excited for me to play it. When I did, I was pleasantly surprised! He had gone to the music studio the previous night, made up a beat, and recorded a track all about the water cycle. He rapped about the water cycle from top to bottom and even gave me a shout out in the rap! Needless to say, 2 things happened. 1. He got an A on the assignment. 2. He got an A on the test for that unit. I can imagine that while answering questions about the water cycle on that exam, he rapped the lyrics to himself in his mind.

My Cheerleader

In addition to being in an alternative certification program, learning how and what to teach, and learning to manage my classroom (as if that weren't enough), I decided to take on being the cheerleading sponsor! I figured, hey, I cheered in high school and college, how hard could it be? I wasn't ready for the time commitment or for dealing with the forty different personalities of the young ladies on my JV and Varsity squads, but the relationships that surfaced, as a result, made it all worth it! I am now friends with several of them. One that comes to mind as having a huge impact on my why and intention as an educator is DeKirsten (image to the left). I will never forget the day she decided that she wanted to give blood in our annual blood drive. She asked me to come and hold her hand as they stuck the needle in and she did the same for me. I'll never forget how on Senior Night, she asked me to walk with her and her mother onto the basketball court as she was recognized as a Senior Cheerleader. What a HUGE honor! Years later, she was a camp counselor and actually took care of my youngest son during summer camp! This December 2018, I will be attending her wedding. I am so thankful that she was a part of my educational career.

My "Pie" Student

And then, there's Cortez (image to the left)! Where do I begin? I had Cortez during his senior year of high school. We started an inside joke and always told each other how "sweet" the other was. So much so, that every "PIE" day, on March 14, we would make it a point to go out of our way to wish each other a Happy Pie Day! It went even further, and every day at 3:14pm we would do the same. All these years later, we try to beat each other and call each other on March 14 to wish each other a Happy Pie Day! Cortez was taking an online class during his senior year and just around graduation time, as everyone was finding out their online class grades, I asked him if he went and retrieved his grade yet. He pulled me to the side and whispered to me that he was scared to get his grade because he didn't think that he had passed. Passing this class determined if he was going to graduate from high school or not. He asked me if I would walk with him to the guidance office to find out if he passed. Once we got there, he told the counselor to tell me his grade and that he didn't want to know. I went into the counselor's office to retrieve his grade. I walked out and looked at him and just shook my head. He kept asking me, "Did I fail?" When we got halfway back to my classroom, I looked up at him (I'm 5'3," and he's about 6'0") and said, "Cortez, you PASSED!!!!" We stood in the hallway, crying and hugging! I will never forget that moment for as long as I live!

Living with Gratitude

The impact of Jermaine's story and the stories of my students has taught me to not only live with intention and purpose, but to show gratitude on a daily basis. There are a couple of ways that I have added gratitude to my daily routine.

The first is to keep a gratitude journal. I purchased a mini Happy Planner from Michael's and keep it on my nightstand. Every night, I write down 5 things that I am grateful for. This simple act forces me to reflect on my day and write down what I'm thankful for. Some days I write down things that are a little more profound, like I'm thankful for waking up, for making a difference in the lives of teachers, for my family and friends, etc. Other days, I'm thankful for a perfect cup of coffee, a peach milkshake from Chick Fil A or a delicious burrito bowl from Chipotle.

***

The second thing that I have done is the 100 Happy Days Challenge. I stumbled across this on Instagram a while ago and decided to try it. I've successfully completed it twice. The first time I did it, I wanted to see if I COULD do it. The second time, I was in a little bit of a "funk" with life and wanted to force myself to take a look at the positive in my life. With this challenge, you are to take a picture of something that makes you happy every day for 100 consecutive days. You then post these images on social media every day with the #100happydays #100daysofhappy. The website www.100happydays also challenges you to create your own hashtag for your challenge as well. Some days I posted a picture of my family, other days it was an ice-cold Coca-Cola! There are no rules except to reflect on your day, be present in the moments of the day, and snap a quick picture of something that makes you happy during the day and post it!

Sharing these gratitude activities with colleagues and friends has spread like wildfire! Several of them have started their own gratitude journals and even completed their own rounds of the 100 Happy Days Challenge. When you take a minute to be intentional about reflecting on your day and finding the good, the happy, and the positive, you become a little more purposeful about what you do every day.

Bringing it all together...My Why

As educators, we get such a limited amount of time to touch the lives of students. In August, when school is back in session, the end of the year seems so far away, but it's not! We have from August to May to impact our students, serve as a positive role model, and help mold them into amazing human beings each and every day. This is such a huge privilege and something that should never be taken lightly. With each day, comes the chance to be 100% intentional and impactful with each interaction we have with our students and our colleagues.

When I think about my students, specifically the ones mentioned about, I am always thankful that I could be in their lives. Yes, even the ones that had challenges. I know that these students were placed in my classroom, during the year that I taught them, for a reason. I am truly grateful that I had the opportunity to not only educate them but to be a positive figure in their lives. I'm even more thankful that all these years later, we still look forward to speaking with each other, catching up, and sharing what's going on in our lives. I am so proud of the positive things that they are doing. In my current central office-based position, often I have to make decisions on issues that will impact students. I often come back and think of these students I've shared the stories of and wonder, how would these decisions impact students like them.

My professional why is for students like Matt, Sheldon, DeKirsten, and Cortez. Being able to experience the pleasure of teaching and making a difference in the lives of my students gives me purpose.

Knowing that I've served even a small piece in their lives that has made them who they are fills me up. My personal why is for my twin brother, Jermaine. Being by his side after his accident, seeing him in a coma, watching him learn how to breathe, talk, and eat all over again was very humbling. This experience has taught me to be intentional with every second of every minute of every hour of every day. Seeing someone you love almost lose their life leaves you wanting to serve others, be extremely grateful, and be purposeful with every moment that you are given.

Bringing together the professional and the personal have molded me into the person and educator that I am today. I make no decisions lightly. If I can't define a clear why as to why I should do something, I don't do it. At the end of the day, if students are not impacted positively by a project that I am leading, I have to question its purpose. When you think of the experiences that have molded you into the husband or wife, son or daughter, teacher or student, principal or superintendent, what was their purpose? How did these experiences impact you? I challenge you to think about each of those experiences and how they contribute to you discovering your purpose and your why. When you've discovered your why, begin to live each day with intention and gratitude. It'll make all of the difference in the world!

References:

Sinek, S. (2009). Start with why: How great leaders inspire everyone to take action. Penguin.

Sinek, S. (2014). Leaders eat last: why some teams pull together and others don't. Penguin.

About the Author

Natasha Rachell

Natasha Rachell has been in the field of education for 15 years. Natasha began her career as a substitute teacher and became alternatively certified through the Georgia TAPP program with DeKalb County Schools. As a result, she earned her certification in Broad Field General Science, grades 6-12. She has served as the department chair in addition to several different committees such as her school's leadership team, the assistant principal selection committee, and the school improvement team to name a few. After leaving the classroom, Natasha took a position with the Department of Professional Learning as the science coach for the Math and Science Transition to Teaching program. Currently, Natasha works for Atlanta Public Schools where she has served as an Educational Technology Specialist and most recently, the Science Digital Learning Specialist. Natasha has immersed herself into the instructional technology space and has earned several certifications, awards and accomplishments, some of which include: Google Certified Trainer, Microsoft Innovative Educator Expert, Apple Teacher, Surface Master Trainer, Flipgrid Ambassador, and Star Discovery Educator. Most recently, Natasha was selected to be a part of the first cohort of Our Voice Academy with EdTechTeam, a group of minority educator leaders from across the nation, sharing their voices with the world.

Mrs. Rachell has furthered her education to earn her master's degree in Educational Administration, her specialist's degree in Curriculum and Instruction, and is currently pursuing her doctoral degree in Organizational Leadership with an Emphasis in Effective Schools. Mrs. Rachell is a recent contributor to Dr. Sonja Hollins-Alexander's, Online Professional Development Through Virtual Learning Communities. She is ecstatic to lead the work as we transition into 21st-century classrooms through blended learning opportunities, BYOD, STEM initiatives, professional learning for instructional technology and digitally connected classrooms. She is a lifelong learner and strives to be the change that she wishes to see.

Making Lessons Memorable

Bonnie Nieves

How I plan to take advantage of schedule disruptions to make my classes unforgettable.

We all know that some activities hit and some miss. It seems a great mystery why some are more memorable than others (the Anatomy Class Halloween lab when students use their knowledge of tissues to identify mystery organs obtained from the butcher shop, the Physiology Class Health Fair where students research a topic of their choice then plan activities and demonstrations for a public health fair, an exploratory science experiences where kids experience science through crime scenes). These are the ones that my students refer back to with satisfaction and fondness.

As I reflect upon my school year, it occurs to me that I have accidentally developed activities which have a blend of specific ingredients that caused them to work. Students remembered them for years to come, referred back to them often as events that helped them to learn, connect with others, and deepen their interest in science. Knowing this, as I plan for next school year, I will use the essential elements of memorable moments. I hope that these scheduled occurrences, although totally intentionally created, will seem like serendipitous moments. I will also remain mindful of impromptu opportunities to harness intrinsic motivation and enthusiasm.

Primarily, I teach Anatomy and Physiology...some people have horrific memories of their experiences in these classes. However, I absolutely adore teaching them. I love the authenticity of teaching and learning about the body that we inhabit and how it evolved to be the imperfect organism that it is. By the end of a semester in my class, I want students to have an increased appreciation for the value of life and have made connections between their experiences in and out of class.

Stepping back to plan, I have identified things that are naturally exciting for students: snow days, holidays, Boston Marathon, Valentine's Day, Halloween, Super Bowl, the World Series. These events break the script of ordinary schedules and sometimes cause distractions. Why not use this increased enthusiasm to our advantage? There are certainly things in my content area that relate to these events. Just to name a few;

- Snow days: hypothermia, extreme sports, homeostasis
- Boston Marathon: heart rate, training, damage to feet and joints
- Valentine's Day: is there a better day to dissect hearts?
- Halloween: appeal to students' curiosity with mystery organs, tissue types
- Super Bowl: concussions and prevention
- World Series: Rotator cuff injuries, hand-eye coordination

With this new mindset, the schedule disruptions that were such a nuisance now are opportunities to create something unforgettable for students. Why not create a folder of plans to pull out for special occasions? Along the idea of sub plans; things to capture the energy of the room and use the enthusiasm to my advantage rather than trying to "talk students down" and coax them into participating in a lesson that they are not prepared to be engaged in.

Another way that lessons have been memorable for students is when they realize their own potential. When students write blogs to set and reflect on goals, they can visualize their learning. I have learned that this is also a method of teaching resilience in students. While I read their blogs, rather than reading to assess the content and grammar I make suggestions about activities for them to try or ways to meet their goals I began doing this because I was honestly interested in who my students are and what they hope to gain from taking my class. I have found that there are not many other teachers who do this; students are surprised that I am connecting the content to their future plans and they can relate to what they are learning. In the end, students have a feeling of accomplishment, satisfaction of a goal reached and a job well done.

When students have this sense of pride, it must be captured and shared. Ordinarily, students present reports and other research to their peers; why not have them recap their journey? Surely there is someone in the audience who will identify with their struggle and appreciate the process and resilience it took to accomplish a goal. The more people share their stories the more we see that we are more alike than different and making stories public is a way to validate and reflect upon the journey.

About the Author

Bonnie Nieves

  Bonnie teaches high school students in Massachusetts. Her professional passions include engaging students in authentic activities, incorporating restorative practices, and leveraging technology to empower students to make an impact on their community. She enjoys connecting with educators through social media, professional organizations, conferences, Twitter chats, and edcamps.

Bonnie is a member of the National Association of Biology Teachers (NABT), the Teacher Institute for Evolutionary Science, the National Science Teachers' Association, and MassCUE, serves as an Elementary and Secondary Education Science Technology and Engineering Ambassador in Massachusetts, and has presented at NABT, the New Hampshire Science Teacher Association, and MassCUE. You can connect with Bonnie on Twitter @biologygoddess, Voxer @bonnienieves, and her WordPress blog Biologygoddesssynthesis.

Between a Rock and a Safe Place

Elford Rawls-Dill, PhD

A personal account of connecting cultural worlds with the intent of building community.

As a pre-teen and teenager, I was cool; at least I thought I was. I grew up in New Jersey on the shore filled with beautiful beaches protected by a 10-foot fence and pay booths designed to keep kids like me from entering and joining the summer fun. The housing project I grew up in was 14 *running* minutes away from the beach. I know this to be true because as a child, I timed my runs to the fence on many hot summer days. On such days, I would leave behind the hectic and sometimes unforgiving concrete environment affectionately called "The Jungle," for the opportunity to peer through small gaps in brown wire fencing, to see how the "others" enjoyed the Atlantic Ocean during the sultry months of July and August. Summer was not mine. The beach was not mine. Even the brown fence that protected the beach from "The Jungle" was not mine. I learned then that physical borders could be erected with the intent to demarcate between individuals, communities, cities, states, countries, and even nations.

The concrete "Jungle" was replete with obstacles and urban stressors that required careful attention and a Zen-like focus to navigate. Corners and streets were crowded with black and brown bodies. There were dice games, crack sales, basketball battles, drill team competitions, double dutchers, and the occasional street fight between rival crews; all on a block in "The Jungle." But even here, deep in "The Jungle," there were old and wise sages that kept us young children safe. These sages, mostly women, would sit high up on porches during the long summer days, sipping from glasses of iced-tea, watching each move we made as we innocently navigated our complicated environment. I do not think I would have made it through the summers of my youth if not for the guidance and positive reinforcement set forth by these *Guardians of the Summer*.

***

During the fall, the beaches emptied but the school doors opened. Summer vacationers returned to their lives and left the beaches and boardwalks vacant and lifeless; this mass exodus was always a harbinger of the start of a new school year. Like the beach, the elementary school I attended was about 15 *running* minutes away from the housing project where I lived. As a child, each year I looked forward to the start of school. Even in my adolescent mind, I identified the start of school as a "rebirth" or an opportunity to "start over" and be a better student. More importantly, school also provided an opportunity to leave behind the worries and stressors of home life. Like the beach, the school was geographically close to the housing projects, but in many ways, it might as well have been thousands of miles away.

There were no brown fences at school, but in many instances, I could easily sense the disconnection between my neighborhood and the place I called school.

It was obvious that many of the adults working in the building did not know about "The Jungle," nor did they realize the sojourn many students took each day to arrive at the doorstep of the school. There were no signs or resembling silhouettes of the *Guardians of the Summer. T*his along with other relational gaps created a culture of "us" and "them."

Over the years, I have often heard an uncredited quote, "when the student is ready, the teacher/mentor will appear." I entered the 5th grade as a hard to tame 10-year-old who had blazed through several elementary school teachers, leaving them thankful and relieved to survive my matriculation through early elementary education. When I entered 5th grade, I finally met the teacher who forever changed my life. Headed for what probably could have been explained as a disastrous educational experience, I desperately needed a teacher capable of meeting me where I "was" while simultaneously challenging me to reach for my limitless potential. A teacher who was confident but also humble; self-aware but also empathetic of the perspective of others, and most importantly, a teacher who was willing to *learn* alongside students with the intention of creating a learning *community*.

With deliberate intention, I will not name "my" life-changing teacher; as I believe it is important that each of you reading this realizes you hold the potential to be a positive influence in the lives of the children you serve. Placing a name to a masterful work of art can defuse the beholder's belief in replicating or improving upon a masterpiece. I am very thankful for my 5th-grade school teacher because of her commitment to nurturing me as a young disengaged learner. Like t*he Guardians of the Summer*, who protected me from social distractions I encountered in my community, this teacher proved to be vigilant in her approach to creating a classroom environment that was physically, emotionally, and socially safe for all students. As a teacher, coach, school administrator, and parent, there are 3 critical elements I hold sacred; I learned each of these 3 elements as a child while under the tutelage of my 5th-grade teacher and the *Guardians of the Summer*. I am forever thankful to them for positively impacting my life and teaching me that...

1. Your words matter.
2. Critical feedback can be life-changing.
3. We are somehow all connected.

Although my *life influencers* never intentionally taught me these concepts, each of their acts embodied a sense of care and a genuine basic belief in all people. I truly believe all educators, both novice and experienced, can benefit from the purposeful implementation of the above concepts.

Your Words Matter

Words are things. Words can cut, bruise, cure, or heal; teachers and adults have the ability to speak positive affirmations into the lives of students. On the other hand, educators (adults) can crush dreams, extinguish hopes, and soften the desires of young people. Teachers possess the power to speak positive affirmations into the lives of children each day. As you read this, reflect for a moment and consider how many opportunities you have during the day to use phrases such as:

- You're brilliant!
- You're on the path to success!
- This class wouldn't be the same without you!
- I made this lesson just for you!
- You have come so far in such a short amount of time!
- I believe in you!
- I enjoy teaching you!
- I learn so much from you!
- You are such a math wizard!

Just imagine the impact these words can have on young people. Even as adults, in our professional and personal lives, we are constantly searching for affirmation. We must remember, the young people we serve thirst for reasons to believe in themselves. Although greatness is within all children, some need more affirmative support to help encourage their path to success both inside and outside of the classroom.

Critical Feedback Saves Lives

I have found over the years that many people struggle with both providing and receiving critical feedback. I have discovered most teachers struggle with this challenge in both the professional and personal setting. On many occasions, adults choose to refrain from giving critical feedback in an effort to remain cordial and maintain *healthy* relationships with colleagues, friends, and family members. My life experiences have led me to believe that effectively prescribing and receiving feedback is a *learned* behavior each of us has the power to optimize. Thus, teachers can engage young people in learning experiences replete with receptive and prescriptive feedback protocols.

Garnering from my own personal and professional experiences, I have discovered many of us are timid when it comes to *prescribing* feedback because we are afraid of an adversarial reaction from the *receiver* of the intended feedback. This can be the case within our own personal relationships as well as the relationships we have with colleagues and students. It is important to realize the absence of critical feedback can result in continued failure and missed learning opportunities for both teachers and students. Thus, a teacher's unwillingness to engage in critical feedback is essentially a symptom of lowering expectations for student development.

Thinking back to my own childhood, I can recall many instances where I failed to utilize sound judgment throughout my decision-making process. My poor judgment usually led to a *sit-down* with my grandmother or my mother. What I remember most about the sit-down is that my grandmother or mother would usually start the dialogue with the phrases:

- *"I'm telling you this because I really love you, and I don't want you to make some of the mistakes I made."*
- *"When I was your age, I wish I had someone to tell me this…"*
- *"You have a future ahead of you, and I want to make sure you make it there…"*

These are the phrases that helped open the portal of my growth and development. I do not recall the mistakes or failures that preceded the talks we had, but I do remember these opening statements. As educators, we are blessed to have the ability to engage with young people each and every day; thus, we have a choice to frame critical feedback with the intent to grow and nurture or dismantle and destroy. My 5th-grade teacher and my grandmother elected to grow and nurture, and their words still remain relevant today.

When prescribing feedback, be sure to reveal your own vulnerability while also voicing a genuine interest in the future-self of the target of your critical feedback. You might have noticed in the phrases above; the prescriber of feedback first inserted their own past-failure into the context of their advice to the receiver. This approach allows the receiver the opportunity to lower defensive dispositions that recipients of critical feedback often experience. Additionally, the prescriber's critical feedback phrases listed above make specific and targeted reference to the recipient's *future-self*. The prescriber's appeal to the receiver's *future-self* serves as an indicator of growth and development. Therefore, the educator's prerogative to utilize target language which references a student's *future-self* helps place the student on a continuum of growth as opposed to the student remaining in the static state of the specific situation which demanded the confrontation.

We Are All Connected

Educators must be obsessed and fascinated with finding ways to connect the dots! Connecting the dots and building relationships help to birth the known from the unknown. Similar to the learning process, building strong relationships requires us to understand how points or coordinates connect and transform simple constructs into complex and impenetrable structures. The moment educators understand the importance of building strong student relationships, they will then witness the metamorphic transformation from classroom to the community.

Like the roles played by the *Guardians of the Summer* in the "Concrete Jungle," teachers who place a purposeful onus on building community have the powerful ability to connect disengaged and disenfranchised students to the learning environment. Such teachers possess an uncanny willingness to soar far beyond the "content" of what they are assigned to teach and into the heavenly realm of creating synergistic learning experiences laden with love, empathy, and sincere admiration for the learner. The truth is, we are all connected; the question becomes, will we foster positive and fruitful connections or connections that are tethered and unproductive?

As educators, we have the best vocation in the world! However, it can be argued that our job is difficult, too. Throughout our careers, we are entrusted with maintaining the physical safety and emotional well-being of countless young people. Not only do we impact the lives of the students we directly serve but we also impact the lives of those people they come in contact with, as well. In a sense, we work on a schedule of compound interest;

our formulated relationships will either build positivity or negativity at an exponential rate. I am suddenly reminded of the brown fence that stood between the beach and the jungle. That fence failed to connect two worlds; it was a dead portal that stunted the potential to build diverse communities. Even so, I will forever be encouraged by the *Guardians of the Summer* and my 5th-grade teacher, who, without a doubt, built bridges and broken-down walls.

This is dedicated to my Grandma Pauline Rawls, my 5th-grade teacher and all the *Guardians of the Summer*. I will always love you.

About the Author

Elford Rawls-Dill, PhD

"I am a life-long learner who is committed to improving the learning experiences for students and teachers."

Dr. Elford Rawls-Dill is a life-long learner. Over the last 15 years, Dr. Rawls-Dill has devoted his life to teaching, mentoring, coaching, and leading both students and staff in the New Jersey private and public school sector. Dr. Rawls-Dill has successfully led the charge to increase student achievement at the school and district level as a school administrator. In addition, as a school principal and district administrator, he has worked to formalize curriculum implementation with a high level of fidelity. During his school administrative tenure, he has successfully led student-centered educational reforms replete with rigorous academic standards and relevant 21st Century learning models designed to enhance the learning experiences for all students. In addition to curriculum design, Dr. Rawls-Dill has also led school and district-wide efforts to develop formative and summative assessment protocols designed to assess the written and taught curricula in the core content areas of language arts and mathematics.

  Dr. Rawls-Dill currently serves as District Coordinator of Curriculum and Instruction for students with disabilities. In his role as District Coordinator of Curriculum and Instruction, Dr. Rawls-Dill mentors school principals and instructional supervisors.

  During his tenure as District Coordinator of Curriculum and Instruction, he has led a district-wide curriculum audit process which included the restructuring of the written, taught, and assessed curriculum in grades Kindergarten through twelve.

In addition to school leadership and curriculum development, some of Dr. Rawls-Dill's research interests include:

- Culturally Responsive Pedagogy
- Mentor/Mentee relationships for at-risk students
- Game-Based Learning
- Adaptive Technology-enhanced learning protocols

Dr. Rawls-Dill earned his PhD in Educational Leadership at Northcentral University in Prescott Valley, Arizona. He also earned a Master's Degree in Educational Leadership at Monmouth University in West Long Branch, New Jersey.

Dr. Rawls-Dill resides in Tinton Falls, New Jersey with his wife, Tiffany, daughter, Laila, and son, Elford Rawls-Dill, Jr.

Parent Engagement

Dr. Michael Milstead and William Jeffery

Leaving no parent behind.

As I reflect on my background and experience as a school leader, I have been extremely fortunate to have served twenty-one years as an administrator in Title I schools. In a Title I school, a substantial number of the student population (over 40%) receives free-reduced lunch, and most come from low-income households. These schools receive financial assistance from the federal government to help ensure that all children meet challenging state academic standards. Students in Title I schools can often be among the brightest and talented in the world. A high percentage of Title 1 students graduate from school on time and pursue some form of post-secondary learning. Countless studies suggest that when parents are involved in their child's education, then learning is enhanced. I have also found that when parents are engaged in school, students are less likely to be absent, more involved in extracurricular activities, possess a high confidence level, have fewer behavioral problems and are positive about their future. It is a widely held belief, however, that far too many parents from low-income households are not involved in their child's education. This phenomenon is also highly supported by empirical research. My career as an educator has taken me down the path of teacher, assistant, associate, and building principal.

I can honestly state in almost three decades as an educator that not once do I ever recall a parent telling me that he/she did not want to help their child to be successful in school. Many have confessed to me, however, that they were never taught how.

I believe that all parents want their children to succeed. Parents of a low-income however, desire schools to lead when it comes to helping them assist their children. It is important for school leaders to understand that there is a myriad of barriers that may preclude parents from low-income households in engaging with their children's education. Working several jobs, no transportation, caring for elderly parents, and parenting younger siblings are just a few. It is equally important that principals construct strategies that will aid parents in overcoming these barriers and become participants in their child's education.

As building principal, here are some things I did to reach out and engage parents in their child's education.

- **Create a welcoming school culture.** It is human nature to want to feel valued and affirmed. Starting from the time that a parent enters the building the climate should feel welcoming and supportive. The staff and aesthetics of the building should display signs of a partnership between the school, home, and community. For example, most Title 1 schools are culturally diverse. The school should reflect this diversity.

- **Refrain from passing judgment on parents.** There have been times in my school where parents have attended teacher-parent conferences in pajamas, a robe and house shoes. I have encouraged my teachers to overlook the dress and acknowledge the fact that the parent cared enough about their child's education to attend the meeting. Most of the times we have no idea what parents are facing daily. Be professional and courteous.

- **Establish a line of communication throughout the community.** Often information sent home to parents by students don't always arrive at the intended location. That is why it is important that information is communicated to parents, via email, telephone, text and phone messages. School information can also be sent to churches and placed in the announcements, community newsletters, sports events, etc. It is vitally important that schools communicate in various forms with parents.

- **Conduct PTO and PTA meetings in the parents' community.** Many of my parents would work two jobs and just did not have the transportation to come to PTA meetings. I would often hold PTO meetings in the main lobby of apartment complexes where my students lived. They appreciated the fact that the school took the effort to reach out to them.

- **Allow the school to be used as a community resource.** At one of my campuses, local social service agencies would conduct English Speaking courses on Saturday for parents. At another school, we allowed an organization to hold financial literacy classes for parents. On one campus, a new church was permitted to use the school on Sundays for services. Making the school available as a community service center encourages parents to become involved with the school.
- **Involve parents in school governance.** Listening to parents and allowing them to feel safe in sharing their views and opinions is another way of building involvement. Involve parents on campus decision-making teams Parents can be a huge advocate in the community for schools.

- **Be visible in the community.** In each school in which I have been principal, I made it a point to be visible in the community. I did things such as visiting local churches, patronizing a local barber shop, shopping in local grocery stores, and eating at restaurants. When community members see the principal being a part of the community, it builds trust.
- **Use Social Media.** Using social media like Twitter, Instagram, and Facebook in education has a negative connotation, but it is one of the best ways to market your school and be in control of your story. Actively engaging parents through social media postings of student achievement and high-quality instructional evidence lets parents know the culture of the school.

Involving parents in their child's education can sometimes be a tremendous task for a school leader. If students are to perform at their highest level, however, it is imperative that parents are engaged in the learning process. Armed with this information principals must be relentless in their approach to identifying, planning and implementing innovative and creative ways to involve parents in schools. As the chief educational officer, the principal has a duty to lead the charge of promoting parents as assets and not adversaries of the learning community. Parents should be valued, respected and treated as partners in their children's education. When schools, communities, and parents work together in the best interest of the child, the outcome will produce a higher performing student with a brighter future and endless possibilities.

About the Authors

Dr. Michael Milstead

Dr. Michael Milstead is an award-winning and accomplished former high school principal with over twenty years of experience providing quality servant leadership to urban secondary and elementary campuses. His long-standing career in educational leadership has allowed him to serve diverse student populations in Texas and Georgia urban school district. Dr. Milstead has worked exclusively in Title I schools and successful lead schools with special needs, bilingual and ESL programs. His teachers and students have achieved national and statewide recognition for exemplary teaching and academic performance. Among Dr. Milstead's many achievements are his nomination and selection as District Teacher of the Year and Secondary Principal of the Year. As principal of Lamar Consolidated High School his students always meet state standards and, on several occasions, done so with distinction. Dr. Milstead believes that Successful principals are resilient in their efforts to seek out and embrace researched based and best practices opportunities that will enhance their effectiveness as school leaders.

William Jeffery

William Jeffery received his Bachelor's degree in Biology Pre-Med and a Master's degree in Counseling Education from Prairie View A&M University. He earned a second Master's degree in Educational Administration from Stephen F. Austin University, where he is currently completing the Superintendent certification program. As a graduate student, he taught adult education classes at Remington College in Houston, Texas, and went on to teach high school science at Houston ISD's Jefferson Davis High School. Here, he pioneered one of the district's first paperless classroom environments and facilitated its first 1:1 classroom. In 2015, he joined the Digital Learning Department in Fort Bend ISD as a Digital Learning Specialist, assisting teachers and mentor teacher with improving student achievement through technology integration. William currently serves as the K-12 Science Coordinator in Lamar Consolidated ISD. Additionally, he curates 14 different magazines through Flipboard EDU, including "Coach Jeffery's: Teaching with Technology," which boasts 47,000-page flips and at least 15,000 viewers this year alone. In his blog on Medium.com, he writes about teaching strategies, technology education, science instruction, and ways to improve student achievement.

Instructional Coaching: The Impact of 360 Video

Crystal R. Morgan

Why 360 Degree Video?

Hamster Wheel

Have you ever watched a hamster in a wheel roam around a room? Every step changes the angle and the perspective for that hamster. The ball gives the pet full access to explore the environment without risks. There is a full way to have full access to classrooms and professional development in the same way.

Jim Knight, the director of the Kansas Coaching Project, is often quoted, "... because of video, we are moving away from a culture of talk to a culture of actions in schools" (Iowa Department of Education, n.d.). Whether the coaching model is *Inquiry-Based, Data Coaching, Cognitive*

Coaching, Content Coaching or Student-Centered Coaching, two common components of the desired coaching model and cycle are observations and post-conference.

Yes, learning standards and quality teacher moves will facilitate progress and measurable student results. This criteria within itself stirs the direction of conversations between teachers, PLC's and Instructional Coaches. A deliverable from this collaboration will yield a rubric or "look fors" during the lesson and observing the captured footage of the lesson.

Traditional Video

During the observation of a lesson, one of the main moves is to script the teacher's directives, questions, and dialogues with students, groups and whole class. Yes, you may have a traditional camera placed strategically to capture a linear focal point that serves as the angle bisector of footage captured on video. The limitation of visibility is determined by what faces the camera. In order to capture as much footage as possible, the camera may be moved at specific times, which can be disruptive to the learning environment at the least.

A positive for traditional video is the ability to zoom in on one specific group to monitor the teacher moves and questioning strategies utilized as a sample of what was occurring across the entire room, hypothetically, with each student or group. This, by definition of sample, is limited data.

Why 360 Video

There is an anecdote that states, "There are three sides to any story: yours, mine and the truth." In education, we can make the amendment to state, "... the teacher, the students, the instructional coach, and the truth." Keeping this in mind, let us go back to the hamster in the reference.

360-degree video places all stakeholders as the hamster in the wheel observing the level of engagement of each individual in the room. Whether you capture a 360 degree picture to analyze a frozen moment of the classroom, or you observe five to eight minutes of 360 degree video of a classroom, all stakeholders participating at the observation stage using the generated rubric or "look fors" from collaboration can then observe qualitative and quantitative data for the levels of engagement of students, teacher moves through questioning and physical location in the room. If you add a digital recorder to capture the audio, this will enhance the data to measure academic language used by all parties.

With live captured data, 360-degree video observations, both the teacher and the instructional coach can have deep, authentic conversations about the student-generated work, and patterns observed from the students and the teacher. Questioning can drive reflection and growth. What empowering behaviors are evident? What limitations exist? What specific barriers are visible?

When viewing the moment in 360-degree footage, every turn reveals more data in the form of what do you see? What was the expectation? Is the table talk/behavior progressing toward an academic goal? Is the grouping promoting positive academic culture? These are just some sample questions that have come from post-conferences, after both the teacher and the instructional coach have watched the footage or as they review the footage together.

360-degree media moves reflection from samples of class data with assumptions that this is the norm for the classroom culture to actual evidence that can be analyzed. 360-degree videos provide opportunities for reflection on how the teacher manages, monitors and modifies as they interact with individual students, groups and the whole class. Teachers are able to plan from a holistic account of experiencing their instructional time. Knowing the intentions and preferences becomes observable and measurable. The teacher and instructional coach grow from the diverse setting and uniqueness of each class.

What to Expect

This yields a more precise and strategic approach for planning and execution. Knowledge of the continuum that exists from a holistic approach opens the capacity for learning over memorization and repetition. Teachers are able to monitor their short- and long-term goals, facilitate increased students critical thinking skills, and measure overall progress.

360-degree video will challenge all stakeholders to close the gaps between planning a lesson and the reality of execution. This will increase emotional intelligence from subjective views, personalizing feedback in with a negative perspective, to communicating objectively allowing each person to keep their emotions under control. 360-degree media will create a culture that moves all stakeholders out of their comfort zones. Everyone becomes focused on growth and accountability with authentic observations, reflections, modifications, and executions.

The partnership created from observing this holistic 360-degree coaching strategy with agreed upon "look fors" will strengthen both the teacher and the instructional coach equally. The culture of action becomes the driving component from reflection.

References

Iowa Department of Education. (n.d.). Retrieved November 22, 2018, from https://educateiowa.gov/

About the Author

Crystal Morgan

As an Instructional Coach, Crystal enjoys supporting the implementation of technology and increasing engagement in classrooms. She enjoys the feeling she gets when teachers begin their transformation from compliant to committed. This is done through powerful coaching conversations, conversations that promote reflection: the greatest instrument to change. This is when she knows she is making a difference.

Crystal has been an Instructional Coach in Dallas ISD for 12 years addressing coherent development of mathematics curricula, learning progressions, and connections across topics and across all grade levels, understanding the role that application, modeling, and contextualization should play, along with associated challenges. She understands that her commitment comes from her calling.

I've Got a Fever, and the Only Cure is More Flipgrid!

David Dutrow

The Need to Amplify Student Voice and Collaboration

In March of 2017, I looked around my classroom and saw a need. I was doing most of the talking in my classes, and that needed to change. While my students seemed comfortable taking notes and occasionally sharing some insight concerning the struggles of Elizabeth Bennet and Fitzwilliam Darcy, I knew *Pride and Prejudice* demanded better of my students and of me. I loved the novel, and I wanted my students to understand why and at least develop an appreciation for it. But as we neared the end of the school year, everyone was tired, and I worried that trying anything new would make them jump the tracks. What we were engaging in then, however, was what some scholars call the consumerism of education. When students consume knowledge and do not create anything, what results is a "changing dynamic between staff and students that makes it more difficult to work together in a reciprocal manner" (Bishop, 2018). I wouldn't allow that to happen. More than anything, I wanted my students working with each other and with me in ways that would become necessary once they moved onto college and the workforce. When I reached the point where even I was getting bored, I decided to take a plunge that has since transformed my classes into vibrant, collaborative, amplified environments. Simply put, I developed Flipgrid Fever.

Catching Flipgrid Fever

When I first encountered Flipgrid at a conference, I was intrigued. In the words of Karly Moura, one of the most respected Flipgrid aficionados, Flipgrid is "a video response platform where users can respond to a prompt and have online video discussions" (Moura, 2018). What drew me to it was its simplicity. If a student had access to any device with a camera, he could produce a short video expressing his thoughts with just a push of a button. Then, the video would be shared with the entire class from anywhere. It amplified student voice, it destroyed the four-walled classroom model, it helped students learn lessons in video production and public speaking, and it gave students the chance to be creative with various filters, stickers, and drawings enabled in the video. As a teacher, I was able to control the students' abilities to reply to other students. To establish trust, build digital citizenship, and limit trolling, I withheld the reply function until students became comfortable appearing on a video. Later, when I saw how many students enjoyed Flipgrid, I opened the more collaborative functions of the platform and students began engaging each other like crazy, in incredibly positive ways. It is not often a new technology fills so many needs, but Flipgrid integrated perfectly into my classroom. What is it that makes Flipgrid such an amazing tool?

Meeting Students Where They Are

Many of our students today are immersed in what Christina Melly describes as a "participatory culture," which essentially is "a community in which there are low barriers to expression, strong encouragement for content creation, and readily available mentors" (Melly, 2018). In short, students are comfortable using tools that allow them to express themselves and create, provided there are guides along the way. Flipgrid insists on students creating, which is what first drew me to it. My traditional means of soliciting student responses was the written word, and as an English teacher, I know there is still great worth in that. But I wanted to know what the students really felt and thought, and their written responses seemed to be hoop-jumping exercises. They did just enough to satisfy me, but that is exactly what I didn't want! Speaking on camera, though common to them with Instagram, Snapchat, and other platforms, wasn't something they had perfected, so we worked on being honest and open and keeping the videos simple. In doing so, their responses became revelations of their thoughts. They rambled at times, but they delved more deeply into the literature when they were speaking their thoughts as opposed to writing them. And since Flipgrid gave them as many "do-overs" as they needed, they could still hone and practice their thoughts, recording them as many times as they wanted before sharing them with the class.

Building and Supporting Creativity

In a blog post entitled "Increasing Student Participation," The Teaching Center asserts, "Ideally, the goal of increasing participation is not to have every student participate in the same way or at the same rate" (The Teaching Center, 2009). And in this area, Flipgrid allows students to respond in their own ways and in their own time. In my first Flipgrids, I asked students a simple question or added a brief video for them to watch, and I asked them to respond to these stimuli. I gave students options so they could create videos that were varied and let them be themselves. As in the classroom, some students were more outspoken and energetic on Flipgrid, but every student found his voice. Unlike the classroom, where students can say "I don't know," or attempt to crawl back into a shell, using Flipgrid gave every student a safe, creative space where they could tinker with the options available to them and produce a response of which they were proud.

More quickly than I thought, students began running with the creativity that Flipgrid allows. First, they found and used the colorful stickers and drawings to make unique portraits. Then, they realized that wherever they recorded was basically a movie set, so they began fashioning what can only be called tableaus behind them, visible to everyone when they watched the video. Each setting was special to the student, so I also was able to learn more about who they were, see what was important to them, and build a deeper rapport than I did just in the classroom. Finally, they began creating themes for the Flipgrids, encouraging their classes to adopt a specific buzzword to creatively insert in the Flipgrid or to wear a certain kind of costume. They were having a blast, and I was receiving videos from all the students. When I used written responses, there were always missing assignments. Using Flipgrid to present students with voice and choice was changing the way they thought about assignments. More than an assessment, Flipgrid videos were something to create and something to experience, and I was learning far more from them than I ever was traditional responses. A 2012 article on student participation perhaps states it most plainly: "classrooms are richest when all voices are heard" (Abdullah et al., 2012). Seeing their creations, I indeed felt like the wealthiest man alive. Not only were my students learning and sharing more, but they were also having fun doing so.

Collaboration Station

Once I had student buy-in, I wanted to leverage Flipgrid for more than just response videos. Flipgrid has powerful collaborative abilities that can take your students' creativity to new levels. Collaboration can be as simple as creating dialogues with Flipgrid, with students responding and expanding on each other's Flipgrids, but they can also work together to produce even greater results. One method I have found useful is the idea of stop-motion. When recording a Flipgrid video, you can pause the recording. In this manner, you can easily change environments and speakers. Multiple students can engage together with one Flipgrid to produce up to a five-minute mini-film. I have found this an interesting way to harness their innovative thoughts to reproduce scenes, chapters, or even poems.

You can use Flipgrid in even more dynamic, collaborative ways, however, and a trip to Twitter can put you in contact with the many experts and Flipgrid Ambassadors out there. Bonnie McClelland (@BMcClelland24 on Twitter) developed the idea of GridPals, which connects classrooms around the globe in a digital pen pals project. Multiple classrooms can connect through Flipgrid and students can collaborate effectively within the grids. If you choose the premium Flipgrid Classroom, there is even a CoPilot function, which gives multiple educators access to the educator dashboard. Flipgrid shrinks the globe and gives educators so many possibilities for connecting classes and working together. While Flipgrid's uses are as limitless as your imagination, Karly Moura's blog post "Ignite a Flipgrid Fire ☐ 15 MORE Ways to Use Flipgrid in Your Class" is a terrific resource for starter ideas (Moura, 2018). For even more ideas, simply search #FlipgridFever on Twitter and see how many educators are changing their classrooms in incredible ways!

Flipgrid for Professional Development and PLNs

As I became more comfortable with Flipgrid, I came to the realization that Flipgrid wasn't great for just my students, but that it could propel my own learning as a teacher. Telecollaboration in the classroom is wonderful, but Flipgrid has become my go-to telecollaborative tool. I've discovered uses for it with parents, with other teachers, and with my personal professional development. Like Twitter, Voxer, and Skype, Flipgrid offers the opportunity to connect with your PLN, and as with my students, its possibilities are only limited by imagination.

Keeping Up with the Joneses (and the Smiths and the Clarks, Etc.)

One powerful use of Flipgrid that I have discovered is the digital parent-teacher conference. At the start of the year, I created a grid introducing myself to parents and provided them with the code to the grid. Whenever they had a question or a concern, they could make a video from their phone or their computer and asynchronously confer with me. My setting permissions on the grid, only I could see their videos, so there was no threat of other parents listening in. As meeting times are hard to schedule with people's busy lives, Flipgrid became the perfect tool for concerns and questions that weren't terribly crucial but when parents wanted quick answers. Being able to see and hear one another gave our online conferences a more personal feel than e-mail, and we didn't have to worry about playing phone tag.

Teacher Trainings

At my school, teachers provide most technology training. Available free time (what is that?!?!) is often the greatest enemy to tech training, and Flipgrid provides an answer for this. Often, questions teachers have about technology can begin to be solved with short explanations, and the five-minute videos Flipgrid offers can be a jumping off point. I don't even have to make videos in Flipgrid. I can create training videos about our LMS or a G Suite for Education tool and then upload it to a grid. After giving teachers the code to view the grid, they can reply with questions or comments, and I can then respond with another video or, if there are complexities, by meeting with the teacher 1:1.

Personalized PD

Like the advent of Twitter chats, Flipgrid offers myriad ways to connect to a PLN and fashion your own professional development. One of the more popular methods I have seen is the Flipgrid Book

Study. Lead by Aubrey DiOrio (@AubreyDiOrio on Twitter), I have joined with a group of passionate educators reading Jimmy Casas' *Culturize*. Each week, we read a chapter, and then we share our thoughts, focused around one essential question, on a Flipgrid. We span the United States, but through our videos and replies, we are connected in ways that go beyond even a Twitter chat. I have gotten to know these educators more personally through seeing them talk about the book, and with the grid code, I can always go back and review what one person said easily.

Other schools have created similar grids where a principal asks a question of the week, designed to inspire teachers or have them reflect, and teachers then reply with a video of their own. Giving focus with a question but allowing teachers the time to ponder the question and film when they can give teachers, like students, more options with voice and choice, and with ideas as simple as this, schools are able to transform the way they conduct PD.

Jen Giffen, in a guest post on Flipgrid's blog, wrote about ten additional ways teachers and schools might better use the platform. If you are interested in more ideas, it is an excellent read and can be found here: http://blog.flipgrid.com/news/2017/6/13/10ways (Giffen, 2018).

No Need for a Cure for Flipgrid Fever

In this hectic world of ours, telecollaboration is a time-sensitive way of connecting to not only students but other educators. Flipgrid has given me the tools to simply and creatively give voice to students, to connect with parents, and to forge stronger bonds with teachers and my PLN. While I know this has sounded like a Flipgrid commercial, it is only because my love for the tool won't allow me to stop recommending it. Having been a Flipgrid Ambassador for almost a year now, I encourage you to review it yourself and see in how many ways it can work for you.

Once you enter the world of Flipgrid, there will be a community of experts at your disposal, willing to help you at any time with tips and ideas. Sean Fahey and

Karly Moura have written and updated *The Educator's Guide to Flipgrid*, a free text that will help you get started (Fahey & Moura, 2018). If you're still hesitant, search on Twitter for #FlipgridFever and see all the varied applications that teachers are using. As educators, the need to collaborate with our students and teachers is greater than ever before, and Flipgrid is an awesome tool that will help you do that wherever you are!

References

Abdullah, M. Y., Bakar, N. R., & Mahbob, M. H. (2012). Students Participation in Classroom: What Motivates them to Speak up? *Procedia - Social and Behavioral Sciences,51*, 516-522. doi:10.1016/j.sbspro.2012.08.199

Bishop, D. (2018). More than just listening: the role of student voice in higher education, an academic perspective. Impact: The University of Lincoln Journal of Higher Education.

Fahey, S. & Moura, K. (n.d.). The educator's guide to Flipgrid, 2nd edition. Retrieved from https://drive.google.com/file/d/1y5jyX7C8pBWNB3yjpl84mhY6a9HcqwR2/view

Giffen, J. (2017, June 14). 10 ways to use Flipgrid beyond the classroom [web log post]. Retrieved from http://blog.flipgrid.com/news/2017/6/13/10ways

Melly, C. (2018). "Can we blog about this?": Amplifying student voice in secondary language arts. *English Journal* 107.3 (2018): 12–18.

Moura, K. (2018, April 30). Ignite a Flipgrid fire: 15 more ways to use Flipgrid in the classroom [web log post]. Retrieved from http://karlymoura.blogspot.com/

The Teaching Center (2009). Increasing student participation. Retrieved from http://teachingcenter.wustl.edu/resources/teaching-methods/participation/increasing-student-participation/

About the Author

David Dutrow

David Dutrow has been teaching English at Mt. St. Joseph High School in Baltimore, MD, for twenty-two years. He is a proponent of student choice and voice and in 2017 became a Flipgrid Ambassador. David loves how technology gives his students opportunities to have their voices heard and works technology into his lessons wherever it supports his pedagogy. In 2018, David was awarded the

Excellence in Innovation award by the faculty of the Educational Technology Master's Program at Loyola University Maryland.

Teach Adaptability, not Apps

Tyler Witman

Are we teaching the latest and greatest thing to show up in the app store or are we teaching how to adapt to new environments, skills, and tools?

Every day, I hear about a new website, app or software that has been deemed the next game-changer in education. With each of these new things I hear about, I keep coming back to one question. Was our game that amazing if something so simple can change it?

Monica Burns (2018) wrote an amazing book recently for the Association for Supervision and Curriculum Development (ASCD) titled *Tasks before Apps: Designing Rigorous Learning in a Tech-Rich Classroom* in which she discusses this exact idea. She explains that "technology's rapid growth over months, not years, is a reminder of how important it is to keep our goals for students learning front and center." Monica goes on to describe how building robust, pedagogically conscious lesson plans ensure that when we do use technology, that it is for the right reasons. I couldn't agree more with this sentiment, and it's what I strive for in my classroom on a daily basis. At the same time, I also realize we need to look at the skills we are teaching our students and how they will use them in the future.

As teachers, it's our job to prepare our students for the future. We are expected to make sure students can survive anything thrown at them. But yet, every day I see teachers and students getting caught up in the hype of something shiny and new. As a community, we must strive to do better than this. As we look deeper into this idea of adaptability, we see that in order to prepare our students for their future, we must think about what that future will look like. Students will compete for jobs in fields that have yet to be created. Students must use tools, apps, and software that have yet to be invented. We, as a community, must learn what it means to prepare our students for this brave new world. But no matter what that world looks like, we must always remember that our students do not need a new, shiny app. Students need to learn how to adapt to the twists and turns of real life.

References

Burns, Monica. Tasks before Apps: Designing Rigorous Learning in a Tech-Rich Classroom. ASCD, 2018.

About the Author

Tyler Witman

Tyler Witman is an Instructional Technology Coordinator in Arlington, Virginia. As an adamant proponent of technology integration in the classroom, he focuses his work with colleagues on building capacity in using technology to enhance achievement for all students. As a member of the EdCamp NoVA planning team, Tyler coordinates social media and marketing efforts to promote the event's ability to create meaningful connections amongst educators. Tyler lives in Alexandria, VA with his husband, Michael, and their French bulldogs, Barley and Basil.

Novel Engineering - Integrating STEM and Literature

Tina Lauer

Creating empathy for characters while developing critical thinking skills.

STEM, the Acronym

You have probably heard the term STEM, meaning Science, Technology, Engineering, and Math. The term was first used by "Dr. Judith Ramaley in her position as the assistant director of the education and human resources directorate at the National Science Foundation" (Chute, 2009). The purpose of focusing on STEM in the classroom is that the world is changing, and our students are going to have different opportunities than we did. It is up to us as educators to prepare our students for jobs that might not even be invented yet. Through a focus on STEM integration, we can do just that!

Recently I have heard people use the acronym "STEAM" with the "A" added for "the arts." And now I even hear "STREAM" with the "R" for "reading" and "STREAMS" by adding an "S" at the end for "social studies." I love the arts, and as a former middle school and elementary school English Language Arts and Social Studies teacher, I do understand the desire to add extra letters to the acronym. However, the STEM acronym was created for a specific purpose. STEM content is necessary for students to be successful in today's ever-changing world and the intention of the acronym is to put a focus on those areas with students. So, instead of taking the focus away from those skills by continually changing the acronym, I suggest that we just increase our focus on integrating STEM into all other subject areas through specific, targeted lessons. STEM integration is the ultimate goal. I hope I haven't offended anyone with my statements regarding the importance of keeping the STEM acronym as it was intended, but if I did, I will hopefully change your mind as you continue to read this article.

What is novel engineering?

One of the focused, targeted lessons I spoke about previously that integrates STEM with English Language Arts is novel engineering. When I first heard the term "novel engineering" a few years ago, my mind heard the word "novel" and thought "new." I was wondering to myself... "what is new about engineering?" I kept hearing more and more teachers talking about this "new" engineering. However, I never did a Google search for it or conducted any other research about the topic and just kept thinking that there was now a new type of engineering that teachers were using in the classroom. It wasn't until I attended the STEM Teacher Quality (STEM TQ) Institute the following year at Washington University in St. Louis, MO that I learned exactly what novel engineering really was.

So... what is it? Well, novel engineering (novelengineering.org), created at Tufts University, is a process of integrating engineering/design thinking and literacy. Through the use of literature (fiction or nonfiction), students participate in engineering challenges based on the problems that arise in the stories. Students get a deep understanding of the characters by using the design process. There are many examples of what the design process looks like, and you can find them all with a simple Google search, but I prefer the Stanford model -- empathize, define, ideate, prototype, test. Notice that the design process is not a linear process, but rather a process that can go back and forth between any of the steps because designing solutions can sometimes be a bit messy and go in different directions than initially intended.

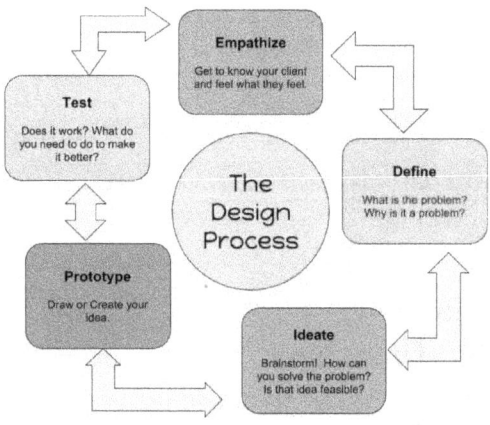

In the first step, "empathize," students connect with the characters in the story they have just read and think about the problems those characters encountered. The characters (or real people in a nonfiction story or article) are the students' clients. They must truly understand the characters inside and out. Close reading is extremely important so that students can understand everything there is to know about the characters in the story and how they feel. They put themselves in the "shoes" of the characters and feel what they feel. You can decide whether you want to use a picture book, novel, chapter or chapters in a novel, article, etc. for the novel engineering design challenge. The Novel Engineering website mentioned earlier has a list of books for grade levels K-8 that are good books to use because they contain multiple problems in which to solve.

After they understand the characters and their feelings, they start defining the problems in the story that the characters must overcome. Most stories have multiple problems within them (even picture books), so students must decide which problem they would like to try to solve. This could be done as a whole group or small group activity. At first, you may notice that students present their design by telling you what the character needed (their design) instead of the problem they were trying to solve. For example, in the novel *A Long Walk to Water* (Park, 2010), the main character has to walk on a path full of thorns and ends up with a big thorn in the bottom of her foot. Your students may say that the main character needed shoes instead of stating the problem which was that the path was full of thorns, she was walking barefoot on the path, and stepped on a thorn. Simple guidance from you as the teacher will not only help one group, but will hopefully transfer to the other groups as well. I do not suggest having students each choose a problem and go through the design process alone. Rather, small groups are ideal for novel engineering because engineering is all about working together to solve a problem. This happens in real life, and we need to prepare our students on how to work together as a team and come to a consensus of which idea would be the best with which to move forward.

The next step is to "ideate" and design a solution to the problem they identified from the story. This is the brainstorming part of the design process. Use of a design notebook is helpful in this step. A design notebook could be as simple as a piece of blank paper or a spiral notebook with ruled paper or as fancy as a notebook full of grid paper. All members of the group should design in their notebooks and label any parts of their design that needs explanation. Then each member of the group shares their ideas with the other group members. This step of the design process brings in the communication skills (listening and speaking) that students need to practice; another way of integrating English Language Arts skills and STEM. After the students share their ideas with their group members, they must choose the solution that they want to create. This is definitely where the communication piece comes in because they have to listen to each other and work together to decide their best option. You could even bring in a decision-making matrix (like the one below) for groups to use when they are deciding on which idea to choose.

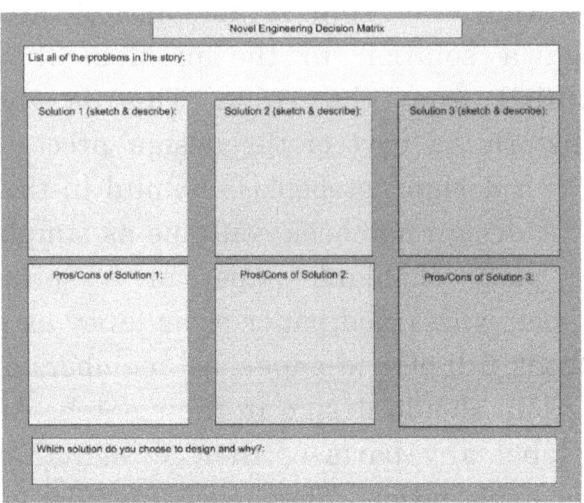

***

If you choose to do so, you can put a stipulation on the designs that they must be a solution that could actually be created in the setting of the story. For example, if the setting of the story is in the 1700s, then a solution of something with electricity is not a feasible solution for those characters. Another stipulation you could put on the designs is that the materials they intend on using with the real design have to be accessible in the setting of the story. Going back to the book *A Long Walk to Water*, a solution that involves making a car to make it easier for Nya to get to the water is not feasible in the setting of the story.

After the brainstorming (ideating), students move into the prototype step of the design process. This can be done a couple of different ways.

- One way is to go full out and use a variety of items to create an actual prototype. Materials to use could include cardstock, paper towel/toilet paper rolls, bubble wrap, boxes, lids, craft sticks, straws, and anything else you can collect. Prototyping is a lot of trial and error as what the students envisioned on paper may not translate completely to the materials they are using to create the prototype. Communication is also key in this step as students work together to create a 3D model of the 2D drawing in their notebooks.

Tina Lauer: Novel Engineering

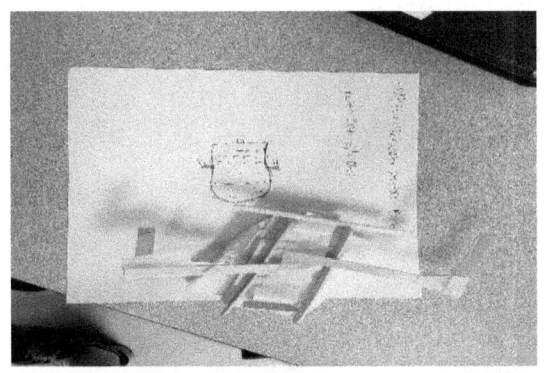

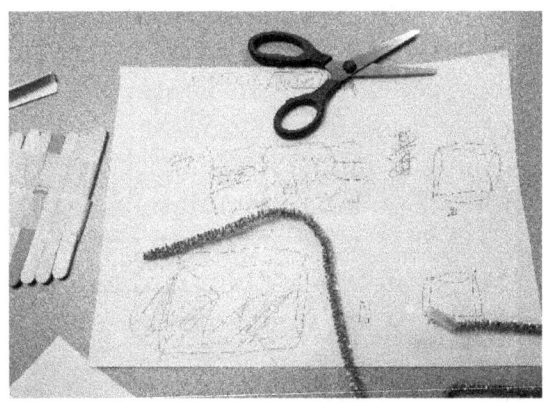

- Another way for students to prototype is on big chart paper. After the group decided on an idea from the previous step, they use a big piece of chart paper to draw their design, label it, and explain in words how the design solves the problem in the story. This way takes less time and is less messy, so it is a good alternative if you are short on time and space.

If students are creating an actual 3D model prototype, they will move to the testing step of the design process to make sure that their design is a viable solution to the problem they are trying to solve. Students may realize that their prototype doesn't work, so they may have to go back to the ideate step and redesign. The design process, as mentioned earlier, can be a messy process where you have to go back to a previous step and try again. Students then realize that they don't need to be perfect the first time. Engineers are never satisfied with their first design.

After students have gone through the design process, it is now Sharing and Feedback Time. Each group presents their design to the whole class. This is an important step in the Novel Engineering process, as it allows each group to communicate to the class what problem they chose to solve and how they chose to solve it. During the Sharing/Feedback session, you should also allow a few people in the class to give feedback to each group. Make sure that you don't always call on the same few people for feedback and limit it to just a few people or your sharing/feedback session will go on way too long. This part of the novel engineering process is extremely important, as it requires all students to be good speakers and good listeners. It will take some practice, but guiding the students in presenting their ideas and giving constructive feedback is key to a novel engineering lesson.

After the feedback session, student groups should be given time to use the ideas they heard during the feedback session to redesign their prototype. This doesn't have to be as much time as the original building time. Students should just be improving their designs during this time, not coming up with a whole new idea.

The final part of the novel engineering process is when the students share their redesigned prototypes with the class. Each group should be given a few minutes to discuss what peer feedback they used from the first share session and how they redesigned their prototype. This will show you as the teacher whether they were able to listen to the feedback given to them and use it effectively in their redesign.

Novel Engineering lessons can be integrated into many subjects. I have used it not only with ELA, but with social studies as well. In our state, Missouri History is one of the state required standards taught in 3rd grade. One of the main focuses of Missouri History is the Lewis and Clark expedition. After reading an excerpt from a book about Lewis and Clark that focused on the setbacks of the expedition, the class went through the novel engineering process and designed solutions to the problems detailed in the book. Through the use of Novel Engineering, students can feel that they are STEM-capable learners and can start to see themselves in STEM-related career fields, which ultimately is the focus of using the STEM acronym and integrating STEM activities into all subject areas.

MakerSpace... the Next Step in Design Thinking

While I have heard many definitions of what a makerspace is, I truly believe that students need to be given time to design solutions to problems that are of great importance to them. This could seem overwhelming to some students at first if they are just told to use the materials in the makerspace and create something. This is why using novel engineering in the classroom can give students an introduction to the design process which they can then transfer to makerspace activities.

A makerspace is the platform provided to students to create. Inspiration occurs in the makerspace. A makerspace should have plenty of materials for students to use for creation. These materials do not have to be very expensive at all, and they can be the same types of materials that you use for your novel engineering lessons. Many schools think you have to have all sorts of electronics in a makerspace and that simply is not true. I have a plastic tub (with wheels for easy transport) full of materials that I have either collected or bought pretty inexpensively. Some of the items include: toilet paper rolls or paper towel rolls, small boxes, cardboard, chipboard, construction paper, cardstock, straws, pipe cleaners, craft sticks, brass fasteners (brads), material scraps, felt, masking tape, scotch tape, duct tape, paper or plastic cups, paper plates, cotton string, ribbon, aluminum foil, bubble wrap, toothpicks, cotton balls, pom poms, wooden dowels, yarn, coffee filters, zip ties, empty cans, empty plastic bottles, scissors, markers, etc. Anything that students can use to build will fit perfectly in a makerspace. If you want to spend a little more, you can add items such as LEGOs, K'nex, Makey Makeys, Little Bits, etc. But, like a said above, those aren't necessary for a makerspace to be an effective place for students to create.

You may have heard the term 20% time or Genius Hour. I'm not sure where I heard those terms first, but it is a trend in education that seems to be catching on. Whatever you do call it, 20% time or Genius Hour, it is where students are given time during the school day to focus on real problems that they want to solve. Many businesses even offer 20% time to their employees. Some of my favorite videos about what 20% looks like in the business world are by Nat and Lo from Google. Check out the Nat and Friends channel on YouTube to see what goes on behind the scenes at Google. Nat and Lo also have a good introduction video about 20% time at Google that I absolutely love. Many of the videos on that YouTube channel can be shown to students to show them that a lot of trial and error goes into creating prototypes, even in the business world.

Offering 20% time or Genius Hour in the school setting may sound challenging to do because of scheduling. It may also be challenging because it does take away from class time. However, you need to think about this time as a way for students to transfer their learning from their classes to a new project. Through research and problem-solving, students use all of the skills they have learned in school to create prototypes that solve real-world problems that are meaningful to them. Students use items provided to them in the makerspace to transfer their learning from the classroom to real-life problems, which is the ultimate goal of education. So, when you think it about it in the view of transfer learning, you can see that you aren't taking away class time for Genius Hour, you are enhancing what is learned in the classroom in another outlet for students to show what they know.

STEM is EVERYWHERE

STEM truly is everywhere! It is in the solutions to the problems in the stories we read. It is in the architecture of our school and other buildings around us. It is in the design of musical instruments we play. It is in the set design of the plays we watch or act in. It is in the digital maps such as Google Maps and MapQuest that we use in social studies and other classes (or to just help us get from here to there). It is in the recipes we use in Family and Consumer Sciences (FACS) class, and so much more. If we intentionally point out the STEM connections in everything we do, our students will feel STEM-capable. They will realize that whatever career field they choose, they will have to use Science, Technology, Engineering, and Math to solve problems that may arise, and they will feel prepared to do so. Remember, we don't need to change the STEM acronym so that every subject area is represented. Instead, as educators, we should be creating focused, targeted lessons that involve STEM into all subject areas so that our students are prepared for whatever lies ahead

References

Chao, G. (2015, May 15). What is Design Thinking? The Stanford Daily. Retrieved from https://www.stanforddaily.com/what-is-design-thinking

Chute, E. (2009. February 9). STEM education is branching out Pittsburgh Post-Gazette. Retrieved from http://www.post-gazette.com/news/education/2009/02/10/STEM-education-is-branching-out/stories/200902100165.

Nat and Friends. (2015, July 13). *Nat & Lo's 20% Project – Go Behind The Scenes At Google* [Video File]. Retrieved from https://www.youtube.com/watch?v=r4UjBNZSXjo&list=RDQMmHpDdo6ZgZI&start_radio=1

Park, L. (2010). A Long Walk to Water. Boston, MA: Clarion Books.

Tufts University Center for Engineering Education and Outreach (2014-2017). Novel Engineering. Retrieved from http://www.novelengineering.org/

About the Author

Tina Lauer

Tina Lauer has been an educator for over 25 years. Currently, she serves as the instructional technology specialist in the City of St. Charles School District in St. Charles, MO. She also is an adjunct professor in the School of Education at Lindenwood University in St. Charles, MO. She is a Google Certified Level 1 and Level 2 Educator, Innovator, and Trainer. STEM integration into all subject areas is her passion. She has presented on various technology and STEM topics at several conferences including the Midwest Educational Technology Conference, MO Summit featuring Google for Education, MoreNET, and the International Society for Educational Technology (ISTE) conference. She is also the recipient of the Midwest Educational Technology Community (ISTE affiliate) Conference Spotlight Educator recognition. You can find Tina on Twitter @tnalau.

READY! SET! GO! How to Create a Multicultural Environment in the Young Adult Library: A Practical Guide for You and Me

Desiree Alexander

Get ready, get set, and let's go on the journey of creating a multicultural environment in the school library.

Many librarians have (or want) a diverse collection of materials and resources that not only have books that represent all cultures in their school, but many more cultures beyond. Librarians may get discouraged because there are so many positive and negative examples of multicultural texts available, it is not always easy to know which are positive. Librarians want to help teachers create safe environments that are multicultural and invite safe discussions. We do not want to just sit there with our great collection of multicultural resources by ourselves; we want our collection and our knowledge to spread around the school, creating embracing and promoting a multicultural environment! As a librarian, I asked, "How do I do this and where do I start?" I realized the answer is it starts with you and me! You do this by getting ready, setting up your multicultural collection (not just books), and collaborating with educators. Take this journey with me as I take the steps to create a multicultural collection in my library and collaborate with teachers to create multiculturally inviting classrooms! READY! SET! GO!

Get READY...

First, I will select my criteria for choosing a variety of multicultural text. This is an important task because when students are only exposed to literature that includes their own race, they view their race and traditions as the norm and exclude other cultures. This includes a majority-minority school. For example, if I have a school of majority African-Americans and only share African-American stories with them, they will not encounter any other culture through literature. Therefore, my most important criteria with my diverse collection will be to make sure every person in the school is represented, while not limiting my texts to only those peoples and cultures.

As a librarian, I know it is unrealistic to think that I will have the time to read every book I want/need to order. However, we cannot order blindly either. To choose texts, I will either read the text or read reviews of the work. It would be great to do both if time allows. I will choose different lengths and genres of works, such as traditional texts, fiction, nonfiction, and poetry because students respond to different genres of print differently. Some students prefer the true accounts of nonfiction, some prefer the form and flow of poetry, and some desire the elements of fiction. I want them to expand their knowledge of people and cultures, and I have no preference as to what form that comes in. Also, different genres show different viewpoints and different aspects of cultures. I will include different texts from the same peoples and cultures because no one text can represent the full diversity of people and culture.

In choosing texts, I cannot solely rely on my opinion of the work because I have the duty of impacting children with this piece of work. I need to be sure that the text is as accurate as possible if I portray it as a positive picture of a people or culture. Therefore, I will have to read critical analysis and talk to colleagues about my text choices. I have had many instances where I felt one way about a book until I read a review or talked to someone in that culture and then felt differently about the text by the end of the entire experience. As librarians, we may not be able to help what is already in our libraries when we step in them, but we can affect what comes in them while we are there.

SET up Your Multicultural Collection

Great authors

Some authors shine bright and are known as the best at what they do. These authors are some of the best of the best (according to my opinion and critics), and hopefully, your collection will include more than one book from each of them. These authors include Joseph Bruchac, Julius Lester, Mildred D. Taylor, Laurence Yep, Sandra Cisneros, Lois Lowry, Suzanne Staples, Ashley Bryan, Gary Soto, Paul Goble, and more. All these authors have exemplary works in various cultures. They all have excellent critiques of their work and produce good, quality work. Their works are thought-provoking and delve into different aspects of cultures. Their works also vary in genre, length, and style. Having works by these authors will be a good starting point for creating your multicultural collection.

Character vs. culture

There are healthy debates about whether multicultural texts should include characters from different cultures in "normal" thematic situations or be a text where characters deal with situations found within the actual culture. Digging deeper, within those texts that deal with the culture of a people, there is also an ongoing debate on whether all representations of a culture are positive. For example, is it enough to call a book multicultural if a character is Hispanic, but going through "normal" teenage situations, such as first love and bullying at school? Some feel that this type of representation is needed because it shows other cultures as being part of the "norm" and does not stress the character's culture. Others feel as this is "whitewashing" because it includes the experiences of the characters teenage trials while ignoring an important part of the character's life: their culture.

Within the canon of books that do represent the culture of characters, there is a debate on which subsection of culture is represented most. For a time, the most popular representation of various cultures was street lit or urban literature. These titles often deal with the gritty realism of street culture. You will find many of these titles in the Bluford Series, Urban Underground, Drama High Series, and by authors such as Coe Booth, Coert Voorhees, Ni Ni Simone and more. Some dismiss these books as guilty pleasures because they are quick reads that deal with what some consider the underbelly of urban culture: drugs, pregnancy, gangs, etc. However, to do so is to dismiss the experiences of some of our students. The mistake that librarians make is **only** including these books as representations of various cultures.

The goal is to have urban stories as well as stories that dig into other aspects of cultures. Many great current authors do this, such as Jacqueline Woodson, Marie Lu, Christina Diaz Gonzales, Kwame Alexander, David Levithan, Malinda Lo, John Green, Sharon G. Flake, and others. Also, a growing trend is to have young adult literature that deals with current events, but from the viewpoints of the affected cultures, such as *Dear Martin*

(2017) by Nic Stone, *The Distance Between Us* (2017) by Reyna Grande and *The Hate U Give (2017)* by Angie Thomas. These types of books can help all students understand the different viewpoints of situations they are witnessing on the news.

Book lists

Anthologies that discuss multiculturalism are good resources for many reasons. These books give criteria of how to choose multicultural literature and provide listings of texts that are recommended and listings of texts that are not. They also provide explanations of discrimination against cultures and describe traits of the culture. This information is usually written in the emic view with an understanding of the culture that is immeasurable. Examples of different types of these texts are Violet Harris's *Using Multiethnic Literature in the K-8 Classroom* (Harris, 1997), Hiley Ward's *My Friends Beliefs: A Young Reader's Guide to World Religions* (Ward, 1998), and Beverly Slapin and Doris Seale's *Through Indian Eyes: The Native Experience in Books for Children* (Slapin and Seale, 1998). These are great starter resources for your multicultural collection. Also, doing research online and finding good websites that can be used repeatedly as a source for choosing multicultural literature is also recommended.

The forgotten groups

I would have Esther Sanderson's picture book *Two Pair of Shoes* (Sanderson, 1990) in my collection. You may ask why a high school librarian would have a picture book in his/her collection. Even though it is a picture book, it is a book that can start a good discussion no matter what level of school library you have. It is a simple story that is extremely relevant to the discussion of the separation and merging of macro- and micro-cultures. Maggie, a Native American girl, gets a pair of patent leather shoes, as well as a pair of moccasins as gifts. She loves both pairs of her shoes and does not shun away from either pair (or either culture). This book can open the discussion of being part of two different cultures and how students deal with that. Think of the discussion the librarian can start by using this simple picture book!

This is the type of genuine discussion students are not getting in our test-driven schools. Sometimes it is up to us, as librarians, to start the conversation!

If you would like to, you could then move to a discussion of Native Americans. Native Americans are still so blatantly stereotyped and discriminated against in America that people often do not realize they are being prejudiced against them (Have you ever "played Indian" or dressed like an "Indian" for Halloween? Think about it!?!). Students can view how rich a culture they have and how their lives are affected by such treatment. Joseph Bruchac would be a star author during this discussion. Bruchac's *Eagle Song* (Bruchac 1997) deals with discrimination and racism in Brooklyn and the main character Daniel rising above it all by learning more about his culture and himself. Using short read can be used to start a discussion about not only this culture, but about institutional racism and privilege is current and worthwhile.

Another group of people that are not discussed very often is the homeless in America. The homeless encompass every race and many of our students, whether we are aware of it or not. Judith Berck's nonfiction *No Place to Be: Voices of Homeless Children* (Berck, 1992) and Eve Bunting's short story picture book *Fly Away Home* (Bunting, 1993) are both texts from homeless children's point of view. Some other cultures that are underrepresented in our school library collections are the adopted, LGBTQ (or LGBTTQQIAAP), special needs and interracial populations. Research should be done to find great titles that represent these cultures.

GO Forth and Collaborate

Storytelling

Now that I have my criteria for how to select my books and I have ordered materials for my library, it is time to start thinking outside of books (a collection is more than books). What can I do as a librarian to start relevant discussions? How can I start collaborating? One thing I can do is invite storytellers to come to my library to share stories from different cultures. If this is not possible because of lack of resources, funding or time, I can purchase videotapes of storytellers sharing stories from different cultures. Novelist Chimamanda Ngozi Adichie's (2009) TED Talk on The Danger of the Single Story is a great place to start to not only understand the importance of a good storyteller, but also to comprehend why we need multiple different stories to represent cultures.

Many teachers may think that storytelling does not fit into the curriculum, but as Margaret MacDonald, renowned storyteller and author of *The Story-teller's Start-up Book: Finding, Learning Performing and Using Folktales*, states that "storytelling teaches listening. It models fine use of oral language. It models plot, sequencing, characterization, the many literary devices you wish to convey. There is no better educational tool to teach language-arts skills" (MacDonald, 1993, 43). Also, MacDonald says, "Sharing story broadens our awareness of other cultures and gives us a deeper understanding of our own" (MacDonald, 1993, 101). Storytelling can begin discussion. Students can tell stories from their culture, their family history or from their lives. They can do this in the library or as an extension activity in the classroom. The teacher can also have students choose a culture and tell a story from that culture (using books and resources from your library, of course). I agree with MacDonald that "it is pretty hard to hate someone whose story you know" (MacDonald, 1993, 104).

"Cinderella Around the World" collaborative lesson

Another collaborative lesson is Cinderella Around the World. It includes Cinderella tales from a variety of different peoples and cultures. This fairytale is represented differently by so many cultures; it really is a fascinating journey around the world. After discussing what the Cinderella tale tells us about the values of that culture, the librarian can collaborate with a teacher to go on a journey through that culture. The students can find different traditional literature, poetry, nonfiction, fiction, videos, and any other resources from and about that culture; then, they can present what they find and tell if it is a positive or negative example of that culture. A listing of the various Cinderella tales can be found in many book ordering catalogs, such as Shen's Books' *Sharing a World of Stories* (Shen Books, 2003). Besides individual books, use Katharine F. Goodwin's *In Search of Cinderella: A Curriculum for the 21st Century* because it is an anthology of 12 different Cinderella story summaries with lessons (Goodwin, 2000). This is a great way to discuss other cultures in an everyday lesson that uses the library's resources extensively.

If these walls could talk

Look around your library! Walk through classrooms! Look at how and if different cultures are represented on the walls and/or in the decorations. A multicultural environment is the first message sent to students that they are accepted in the school. Before anyone in the library or at your school speaks to a student, they see the walls, the decorations, and the surroundings. However, just as in texts, decorations need to be chosen carefully. Make sure different cultures are represented respectfully. For example, is a Native American referred to as red, Indian, or grossly surrounded with symbols? Does the "I" in the alphabet stand for "Indian?" Is the skin color, hair texture, or facial features of the African-American children over exaggerated? Are the Spanish American children seen working in stereotypical jobs? These things need to be analyzed because having a multicultural environment sets a tone without words.

Never Stop Learning

The importance of creating a multicultural collection in your school library is crucial. You can be **the** person at your school who provides the resources for students and teachers to open the critical discussions that are so desperately needed in schools. Our multicultural collection could serve two purposes: for our students to gain the knowledge and have the experience necessary to form intelligent opinions about society and for educators to do the same and actively use and spread that knowledge in their classrooms and lives. Hopefully, we can motivate and influence our teachers to go beyond the superficial when discussing other cultures (food, clothing) and use multicultural materials during everyday lessons. Reading and using multicultural books during lessons is an effective way to incorporate "other" cultures and make them part of the "norm." It demystifies cultures as "the other" and makes them a valued and relatable part of everyday life. We can also help teachers learn and use the tools of choosing multicultural materials that represent cultures accurately and with respect. I am expecting our multicultural collection and knowledge to have a long-lasting impact that will continue to touch people's lives long after us all.

References

Adichie, C. N. (2009, July). *The danger of a single story*. [online] Retrieved from https://www.ted.com/talks/chimamanda_adichie_the_danger_of_a_single_story?language=en

Berck, J. (1992). *No place to be: Voices of homeless children*. Boston: Houghton Mifflin.

Bruchac, J. (1997). *Eagle song*. New York: Dial Books for Young Readers.

Bunting, E. (1993). *Fly away home*. Boston: Houghton Mifflin.

Goodwin, K. (2000). *In search of Cinderella: A curriculum for the 21st century*. Fremont, CA: Shen's Books.

Grande, R. (2017). *The distance between us*. New York: Simon & Schuster.

Harris, V. (Ed). (1997). *Using multiethnic literature in the K-8 classroom*. Norwood, MA: Christopher-Gordon.

MacDonald, M. (1993). *The story-teller's start-up book: Finding, learning, *performing and folktales.* Little Rock, AR: August House.

Sanderson, E. (1990). *Two pair of shoes.* Canada: Pemmican.

Shen's Books. (2003). *Sharing a world of stories.* [catalog]. Fremont, CA: Shen's Books.

Slapin, B. & Seale, D. (Eds.). (1998). *Through Indian eyes: The Native experience in books for children.* Los Angeles, CA: University of California, American Indian Studies Center.

Stone, N. (2017). *Dear Martin.* Toronto, ON: Crown Books for Young Readers.

Thomas, A. (2017). *The hate u give.* New York: HarperCollins.

Ward, H. (1998). *My friend's beliefs: A young reader's guide to world religions.* New York: Walker and Company.

About the Author

Desiree Alexander

Ms. Desiree Alexander, Ed.S. is an award-winning, multi-degreed educator who has been in the educational field since 2002. She is currently the Regional Director of North Louisiana for the Associated Professional Educators of Louisiana. She is the Founder CEO of Educator Alexander Consulting, LLC. She consults with members of several schools/businesses and presents at conferences nationwide.

Ms. Alexander is lifetime certified in Louisiana in Secondary English Education, as a Reading Specialist, as a School Librarian, as an Educational Technology Facilitator, as an Educational Technology Leader and in Educational Leadership 1. She is certified in Texas as a Principal, in English Language Arts and Reading for grades 4-8 and grades 8-12, as a Reading Specialist for grades EC-12, and as a School Librarian. She holds multiple technology certifications, including, but not limited to, IC3 certification, Google Certified Trainer, Google Innovator, Apple Teacher 2016, and a Microsoft Innovative Educator Master Trainer.

She holds a Bachelor, a Master + 30, and an Education Specialist Degree in Curriculum and Instruction from Louisiana State University. She holds a Master of Library Science from Texas Woman's University. She holds a Master of Educational Leadership with a concentration in Educational Technology Leadership from Nicholls State University. She is currently pursuing a Doctorate in

Education with a concentration in Educational Leadership from Lamar University.

She is one of the 2017 Young Professional Initiative 40 Under 40 Awards Honoree, 2017 Center for Digital Education Top 30 Technologists, Transformers & Trailblazers, 2017 PBS Learning Media Digital Innovator for Louisiana, 2016 A+PEL Member of the Year, 2015 Librarian of the Year for Louisiana Librarian Association, 2014 Leader of the Year for Region 2 Louisiana Association of Computer Using Educators, and her recent campus's 2015 Teacher of the Year in the Zachary Community School District.

Learn more at www.educatoralexander.com.

Using Social Emotional Learning (SEL) as the Rudder to Navigate the Way

Susan R. Mosley

Students learn best when we address emotions in the classroom: Using SEL in the classroom to teach the most reluctant learners.

> "Educating the mind without educating the heart is no education at all." Aristotle

Is it possible that Aristotle understood the importance of Social-Emotional Learning all the way back in Ancient Greece? If he didn't, he was certainly spot-on with his thinking especially when it comes to educating at-risk students.

As a teacher who has been teaching at-risk students and students with significant behavioral and emotional issues for over thirty years, I have come to realize that you have to reach them before you can teach them. One way to reach them is connecting to their heart, and one pathway to get there is through Social-Emotional Learning.

Social-Emotional Learning is a fairly new term in education, and many are unclear about its meaning.

Social and emotional learning (SEL) is the process through which children and adults acquire and effectively apply the knowledge, attitudes, and skills necessary to understand and manage emotions, set and achieve positive goals, feel and show empathy for others, establish and maintain positive relationships, and make responsible decisions (Collaborative for Academic, Social and Emotional Learning [Casel], 2018).

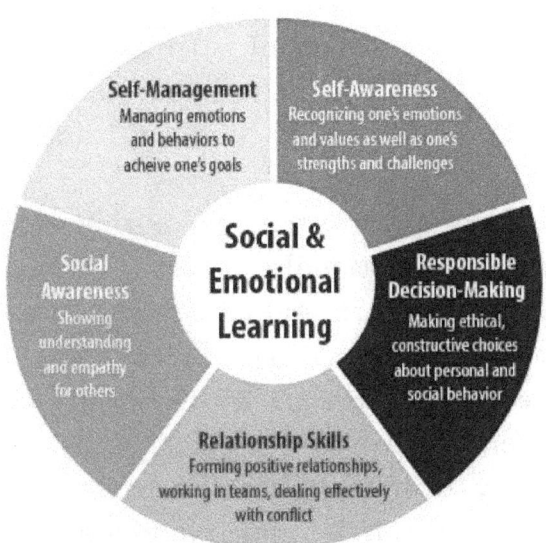

Focusing on the five SEL competencies of self-awareness, self-management, social awareness, relationship skills, and responsible decision-making allows for educating the whole child. Many students come to school with an "invisible backpack" that weighs them down and renders them unavailable to learning. As educators, we need to recognize that many of our kids have arrived in our classroom with issues of poverty, abuse, neglect, or abandonment in their "backpack." It is our job to help students to feel safe and secure in the classroom environment using trauma-informed practices as well as supporting the emotional link to form a bridge to learning.

Emotions are the rudder that steers thinking. Emotional states influence motivation to learn and perception of tasks (Immordino-Yang, 2007). Students who are weighed down (think of their invisible backpack) with heavy emotional baggage will view everything that occurs in the classroom through that emotional lens. Additionally, for learning to transfer from teacher to student, they need to form emotional connections to what's being taught.

How do we form emotional connections to learning? The most effective ways I have found are by providing the following:

- A safe and secure classroom environment
- Forming meaningful relationships with students

- Trauma-Informed Practices in the classroom which includes mindfulness and morning meetings
- A curriculum that integrates Social-Emotional Learning across all academic areas
- HOPE

Safe and Secure Environment

- Showing compassion by avoiding power struggles
- Letting students know you understand their situation and support them
- Providing structure and predictability whenever possible
- Focusing on building trust
- Communicating expectations in a clear, concise and positive manner

Relationships

- Love them: There is healing power in an adult who cares.
- Don't judge.

- Listen with a heart of compassion.
- Give each student a clean slate each day.
- Encourage student strengths and interests.
- Find ways to connect through music, a nickname or a special handshake.

Mindfulness and Morning Meetings

- Start each day with some type of morning meeting or emotional check-in. You can circle up or do a Google form and allow students to check in with you privately.
- Teach mindfulness as a tool for emotional regulation.
- I start with "Mindful Mondays" and then build on that.
- Teach students that "deep breaths are like little love notes to your body."

- Model mindfulness in class. I like to play "hang drum" music in class when we are writing. It is very calming.

Social-Emotional Learning Curriculum

Why SEL matters:

- 83% of students made academic gains when participating in an SEL program with an academic component (Casel, 2018).
- SEL programs improve behavior and attitudes toward school and prevent substance abuse.

Hope

> "Hope is being able to see that there is light despite all of the darkness."- Desmond Tutu

- Cultivate your students' dreams in class: help them to visualize a path to their dreams.
- Give them a voice and a choice in all aspects of the class.
- Believe in them.
- Provide relentless encouragement.

Social-Emotional Learning encompasses so many aspects and can easily be integrated across all academic areas. It is a vital and essential avenue to reach our students who need us the most. Students must be available for learning. Connect heart-to-heart and watch even the most reluctant learners be emotionally available to the learning process.

References

Collaborative for Academic, Social and Emotional Learning (2018). Retrieved from http://casel.org

Immordino-Yang, M. H., & Damasio, A. (2007). We feel, therefore we learn. *The Jossey-Bass reader on the brain and learning*, 183-198. Retrieved from https://onlinelibrary.wiley.com

Susan R. Mosley: Using Social Emotional Learning (SEL) as the Rudder to Navigate the Way

About the Author

Susan R. Mosley

Susan Mosley is currently a Special Education teacher for the Middletown School District in Middletown, NJ. Her career spans over thirty years as a Special Education teacher and has included teaching at-risk youth and students with significant behavioral challenges.

Named Thorne Middle School's Teacher of the Year in 2013, Susan's vast knowledge, experience, and extraordinary leadership skills have allowed her the opportunity to serve as a mentor, building relationships with novice teachers, providing district-wide professional development and initiating programs for at-risk youth including a school-wide mentoring program. In addition, she has presented programs to the youth at the Ocean County Youth Detention Center, is a Newsela Certified Presenter and has presented at numerous educational conferences.

Susan is co-owner of Innovative Educational Practices and Solutions (ieps4bd@gmail.com) and consults with school districts in the areas of Social-Emotional Learning, Trauma Informed, and Restorative Practices. Susan holds her Bachelors in Special Education from Millersville University of PA, her Masters in Special Education from Old Dominion University and her Supervisor Certificate from Georgian Court University in NJ.

Confessions of a First Year Computer Science Teacher

Stephanie Filardo

Last year, students taught me more about what it means to teach computer science than I taught them.

I believe the most important part of my job is to **facilitate problem-solving** and create opportunities to **develop project management and communication skills**. I believed this as a special education and math teacher, and it holds true now that I teach computer science.

Last year, students taught me more about what it means to teach computer science than I taught them. I'm going to repeat that, and I want you to let that sink in for a moment. My students

Stephanie Filardo: Confessions of a First Year Computer Science Teacher

taught me more about what it means to teach computer science than I taught them.

If that sentence makes you uncomfortable, then you have something to gain from the next few minutes of your time. If that sentence doesn't make you uncomfortable, then you may be a computer science teacher.

While we teach many students, this is the story of three of them.

All of us have a **Jake**. He came in thinking computer science, specifically Web design, was the career for him, but discovered that it wasn't. There was a sense of sadness and frustration with this. The next words I told him were some of the most powerful Jake would hear from me: "Knowing what you don't want to do is just as powerful as knowing what you do," **Jake taught me that my classroom was a safe space where we learn and make mistakes. Every kid needs a space like that.**

Our **Patrick** was the quietest student in class. He didn't want to work in partners, and he didn't want to present in front of the class...and yet, *during his second session in my course*, I invited him to share his projects at our innovation showcase at our local ISTE affiliate (METC) conference. He accepted and did an amazing job. While not all students will feel more confident speaking to strangers than classmates, **Patrick reminds us to seek out ways for our introverts to share.**

Urban is the student we are afraid of. He walks into our classroom with more knowledge than can be contained in the curriculum. He is mostly self-taught, so there are gaps in his learning, and we have to figure out how to balance challenging him with the needs of the rest of our class. **Urban forces us to recognize our weaknesses.** We don't know everything. I don't know everything. How do I teach him? What do I teach him?

(You have listened and heard me describe these three very different boys, and possibly you're thinking, "What about the girls?" The simple answer to that is to say that my school is an all-boys Catholic high school. Having said that, some might even question the relevance of anything I would share with you since I teach the "majority demographic" in computer science. So, to those who ask, "What about the girls," I now answer a question with a question. **"What if I'M the girl?"** What if I'm the girl these boys learn computer science from? What if I'm the female management they work under and learn project management from?)

Stepping out of my content area and into computer science opened up a world for myself as well as my students. It was quite possibly the scariest thing I have done, and it has only inspired me to learn more, often alongside my students.

Learning is the journey, while there may be a final product, it's all about the journey. There is something to be learned by all teachers here... How can giving up being the smartest person in the room result in increased student learning and engagement? How do the risks we take make us better? How do we inspire the Jakes, encourage the Patricks, mentor the Urbans, and not forget sometimes the Stephanies are the teachers too? What can our students teach us?

EDUMATCH® SNAPSHOT IN EDUCATION (2018)

About the Author

Stephanie Filardo

Stephanie Filardo is an #ISTE Ignite Speaker, Google Certified Trainer and Innovator, Nearpod Author, #EduSnap16 and #EduSnap17 contributing Author, and METC PAC (Planning and Advisory Committee) member who teaches technology/computer science classes at St. John Vianney High School in St. Louis, Missouri. She previously taught math and special education at the elementary, middle, and high school levels. Stephanie uses technology to differentiate and take new approaches to the curriculum. She enjoys helping teachers solve problems and rethink their classrooms using technology. Stephanie tweets @i3algebra and blogs i3algebra.blogspot.com.

The Creative Teacher

Marvia Davidson

Bring your whole self to the classroom: A story about weaving creativity throughout instructional practice.

How it All Began

I heard it again: *"Ms. Davidson, what are you on? You're so weird."*

The student didn't mean me harm nor insult. He genuinely wanted to know what made me tick and what made me so different from his other teachers.

I replied, *"I'm not on anything. This is 100% Ms. Davidson."* It was me being me.

Other times I would hear students say, "Ms. Davidson, you keep reading. You act it out. You make it interesting and easier to understand. I like the way you read."

Sometimes I would give in, and many other times I would tell students to make a cast of characters as they read to themselves, so they could imagine the voices, emotion, or scenes being played out.

Over the years, personally and professionally, I've held on to those words of "me being me." I have also held on to the idea that none of us can pretend to be otherwise. In teaching, I have had many opportunities to bring my creative side to the instructional space, sometimes with planned intentionality and other times by complete serendipity. I strongly believe it is important to bring your whole creative self to the classroom because it makes you real, relevant, and more connected.

Just Be Real

If you can't be real, and I mean gut-level honest in teaching, then that can make it harder to connect students to their learning. In my own experience, when I made it a point to learn about my students and their likes, dislikes, or interests, it gave me fodder for building learning connections with them. After all, the classroom and instruction didn't just belong to me. It belonged to my students as well. Lessons went better when I got to know them and allowed them to know me too.

To be real means acting from a place of integrity, grace, hope, and dealing with the ups and downs of life. It means owning up to mishaps and things going wrong. It means practicing empathy and compassion. It means making things right with students when a situation goes south. It means letting them know you, too, are human. We can use that humanity - particularly our quirks and foibles - to bring creative nuance to the instructional work we do.

Marvia Davidson: The Creative Teacher

Creative Connection

Building connections with students sometimes requires creative thinking, and I have found many times I was able to connect with a student by referencing or bringing into the conversation things that had nothing to do directly with teaching high school English. Baking, drawing, graffiti, tattoos, creative writing, making art, gangs, having a job, staying out of jail, parents in prison, losing loved ones, addiction, having babies, or working on cars were conversational connections between my students and me. These were things happening in their young lives.

I got to know the real them, and it helped me be a more effective teacher. I would try to relate the instruction to their reality, what they hoped and dreamed for themselves, or what made them light up. When you bring your whole self to the classroom and invite your students to do the same, it can change things for the better. I encourage you to create space for safe and creative connections with your students. Don't be afraid to know the real them because they are all worth it! Being real can also bring a sense of relevance to our classroom work.

Creative Relevance

I taught for over ten years and worked with students from various backgrounds. In much of my lesson planning, I used data to improve student learning and access to understanding challenging texts or modes of writing. I knew early on in my career that focusing only on passing high-stakes exams would not create a love of learning, nor would it benefit my students who were struggling to even make it to school. I had to make learning relevant and fun. To be honest, I didn't begin my teaching career this way. When I first began, I was glued to the skills and objectives with little flexibility. That lasted all of about a year, and I learned I needed to make those objectives fit into how my students learned without compromising school and district expectations. I had to make it fun, interesting, and creative; but I had to do it in a way where students could access and practice the skills they needed, without it being so challenging that they would quit. Relevance became part of the currency of my instructional practice, and was one of the first things I considered when planning. I was able to see the fruit of that relevancy practice later in my career.

I was in my 12th year of teaching when I had a class that was a majority of young men. The lesson I was going to teach was on rhetoric, persuasive writing, and analysis. It was a challenge to teach let alone for my class to understand and learn. I tried the suggestions in ancillary materials and books. Unfortunately, what I was doing wasn't working to teach my students the cerebral nuance of rhetoric, ethos, pathos, and logos. My canned examples were not connecting with them at all. They were getting stuck, and they didn't seem to understand which led them to become flustered. I finally decided to try something out of the ordinary to help the students make connections and develop critical reading, thinking, and writing skills. Rather than use only text for rhetorical analysis, I opted to use commercials (from TV), cereal boxes, edible products, and varied print advertisements targeted at a variety of audiences. The goal was for students to analyze the subject, the audience, and the message by using what was current and relatable. Who can't relate to a box of Froot Loops, a cardboard canister of Oatmeal, a pack of Ramen noodles, or a bag of Cheetos? To bring creative relevance is to bring into consideration what your students bring to the table and adapting the lesson around who they are and what they can relate to.

Once students were able to see the subtle and not so subtle messaging used, they were able to see how they were either being manipulated to purchase or to not purchase a product or engage an idea. I had found a creative way to make it relevant and engaging. I don't think those students will ever look at a box of cereal the same again. This much I know, once we had a better foundation and understanding of the objectives, I was able to add political cartoons and short texts to the mix for rhetorical analysis. My students' skills improved, and they genuinely participated in class. It was one of the highlights of my teaching career. I was able to use my creative skills to improve instruction and learning.

Outside the Box

The best thing about taking that one creative turn was how it opened up possibilities for the young men and women in my class to show off their new skills throughout the rest of the school year. They exceeded my expectations and their own. This kind of bridge building helped my students connect to learning more deeply and relevantly. I understood how important it was to think far outside the box when it comes to making way for all students to access the skills they need.

The creative teacher is one who can bring the whole self to the work - heart, mind, quirks, foibles, flexibility, and creativity. I firmly believe when you bring the whole, real you to the classroom, it keeps you grounded in your passion for the work and personally connected to the work.

Let's not be afraid to weave creativity and the story of who we are throughout our instructional practice.

About the Author

Marvia Davidson

Marvia was a high school English teacher for over a decade in public, private, and charter schools in Texas before becoming a campus administrator. She is currently serving as a district-level instructional coordinator. She has worked with students and teachers from diverse backgrounds and loves helping students realize their potential. She has a keen interest in mentoring teachers and helping them be the best they can be in their work. She believes in taking creative instructional risks that allow students to access their own skills and abilities. For her "think outside the box" means to get to know what makes your students light up, but also remember what makes you light up because that passion can power you through the challenges of teaching. As a lifelong learner, Marvia loves growing her PLN, CoffeeEDU meetups, and collaborating with other educators on how to do what's best for students and teachers. She's not only an educator but an avid mixed media artist who enjoys lettering, painting, and baking. She is committed to learner and teacher development. Connect with Marvia on Twitter, Instagram, LinkedIn, and Voxer. You can also find her writing, making, and creating on her site at marviadavidson.com.

4 C's of 21st Century Learning

David Lockett

The 4Cs: Creativity, Critical Thinking, Communication, and Collaboration.

For some students at Edward W. Bok Academy South, the start of the school year took on the flavor of an out-of-this-world experience!

The school participated in the "Space Docking Challenge," a team project that helps simulate how astronauts move from their rocket to the International Space Station as a pilot navigates their space vehicle to a docking port.

David Lockett: 4 C's of 21st Century Learning

Image courtesy of David Lockett

Students worked together to move a PVC ring with a ball balanced on top (the astronauts) to dock with a larger ring (the ISS) placed on the ground. Like the dual joysticks that astronauts use to control the space station's Canadarm2, students must move in harmony with each other and follow a precise and carefully-planned sequence or the docking process fails.

It wasn't as easy it might have first looked. Our students had to use both mental and physical skills to make sure they could successfully complete their task, which is why this was such a nice back-to-school icebreaker for everyone. The difficulty of the task was easily adjusted for students' abilities by lengthening or shortening strings or using a lighter or heavier ball.

Because our location is not far away from where NASA conducts launches, it's particularly relevant and exciting for our students to relate their learning to space. The space program is continuing to prepare to explore new frontiers in the coming years, and we want our students to be a part of those new missions.

About the Author

David Lockett

    David Lockett is a science, technology, engineering, and mathematics (STEM) teacher at Edward W. Bok Academy, a charter school for grades 6-8 in Lake Wales, Florida.

The 3 Ps and 3 Es

Craig Shapiro

With these as your guide, great teaching is possible!

So, let me challenge you to take a second and think about the educators who positively impacted your life. Have you considered the qualities that made them special? You might remember them for their humor, rigor, organization, or great attention to detail. The key is that all of those teachers had certain common qualities that made them special. As I was writing this, there were moments where I had to think long and hard about what qualities students thought I had, and which ones needed to be developed. That reflection helped me come up with the 3Ps and 3Es. They are Passionate, Patient, Persistent, Empowering, Empathetic, and Enthusiastic. While there are definitely other qualities that make an outstanding teacher, hopefully, you'll agree that the 3Ps and 3Es listed are a great start.

The take away before reading about each trait is simply that any person working with children or teens who exhibits these qualities is making a huge difference in the lives of their students. They are helping them to see the power of learning. They are inspiring young minds to be confident and leaders of the world. Finally, they are what I call "world changers!" That's a person who through their actions and words is making our world a truly better place! I hope you enjoy them!

1st P - Passionate

> I define **passion** as "a strong feeling of enthusiasm or excitement for something."

I've started with this 1st P, simply because being passionate about the job of educating students, is in my mind, the number one prerequisite for outstanding teaching. It's hard to imagine any teacher who gives their heart to kids every day who isn't passionate about what they do. Some might say that passion can't be taught, but I do believe that with practice and a strong sense of purpose, developing passionate energy and love of education is very possible with lots of reflection and hard work. Speaking with thousands of kids and asking them to reflect on how a passionate teacher makes a difference in their lives is the most valuable explanation of its importance.

My high school Spanish teacher, Mr. Black, was the epitome of "the Passionate teacher." His passion for teaching showed in everything he did. Entering the room, you were always met with a smile or greeting. During class, his energy level never dropped. Even in those instances where kids (meaning me) didn't understand the content, he always took the time to address my needs, and more importantly, he did it with true happiness and kindness. For Mr. Black, showing his passion was never hard!

There are two steps that I'm going to highlight for this particular writing. These two will really make a difference if you give them a try.

1. The first step is completely accepting and embracing the impact you have on students each day. Mr. Betz, who was my 5th-grade elementary school teacher had such a passion. He looked like a "hippie" from the Rolling Stones era! His demeanor and kindness were always known by every student. I can't recall any time when he came into class miserable and angry. Even when some of us weren't the best behaved, he still offered encouraging words and an enthusiastic pat on the back. I recall on many occasions that he'd sit me down and just chat about the positive examples he'd hope I'd give to my peers. Obviously being a 5th-grade boy, I didn't always apply those principles. But instead of giving up on me, there was this continuous passion for making a difference in my life and the lives of other students.

Simply put, he made me want to be a better person. Yes, I know that sounds crazy coming from a 5th-grade mind, but looking back, he was a "game changer" for how I acted during that year and on other occasions.

2. The second step is understanding and applying what I call the "wow, this is so much fun" mantra. Let's face it, we have challenging jobs that truly demand our best each day. Because of those challenges, it's easy to see the glass as half empty. If instead, we take the approach that students need me at the top of my game; happy, positive, energetic and excited to teach, then that passionate side starts to shine through.

Part of developing a passionate teaching personality is making an effort to see and experience the benefits of having fun at work. The importance of our mindset and student-centered thinking will help us to be mindful of our students even when we are facing difficult days. Yes, this will take practice and lots of reflection, but over time, it is possible to become a Mr. Betz or Mr. Black of your classroom.

2nd P - Patient

> I define **patience** as remaining calm when dealing with a difficult or annoying situation, task, or **person**.

When I was in college during my freshman year, I'll readily admit that my maturity level was somewhere between "partying with friends and skipping the 8:00 a.m. class!" Luckily, I was fortunate to have Mrs. Gold as my Calculus teacher. During one particular bout of immaturity, my friend and I were having a laughing fit in her class. It's one of those times where even just hearing them giggle forced you to start laughing again. Mrs. Gold witnessed this first hand! Instead of getting upset and being reactive, she actually asked us if we were okay and if we needed to go out into the hallway to catch our breath. Even today, I'm still struck by her level of patience and willingness to actually help us see the bigger picture.

Developing patience, like most other teaching habits, is all about practice and preparation. There will be instances where you're caught off guard by a situation, but more often than not, those that read both verbal cues and both language of students can often nip a situation in the bud. Being aware of smiles, frowns and conversations as kids enter can be a huge difference maker. Of course, when a situation does arise, taking some moments to think about how you'll react is often a very positive way to deal with possible problems. Here are a few ideas that may help your patience win over students:

1. Take a deep breath! In those times where you feel frustrated or angry, taking a few seconds to stay calm can do wonders for a situation. Not only can it de-escalate a possible problem, the ability to show poise won't be lost on your students. They'll admire your patience and may even follow your lead.

2. Remember your audience is kids. We are dealing with students. It's unrealistic to think that most children/teens will have the thinking capacity that we have. Instead of reacting, try to choose words that are calming, positive, encouraging and understanding on what the problem might be.
3. Always remember the end game! In any difficult environment, we always want to avoid the escalation of a problem. Some issues are unavoidable. But most times it's our actions and words that will either win over the student or cause them to become angry.

Being patient isn't something you can learn in a college class, and it's rarely mentioned during your teacher training. But it is something you will develop over time if you truly desire to connect with your students.

3rd P - Persistence

> **Persistence** is the ability to stick with something. (Vocabulary.com, n.d.)

This final "P" is often what I think about during many of the coaching experiences I've had and witnessed from others. Early on in my career, I was lucky to be surrounded by outstanding coaches who always "persisted" on being positive and never giving up on their athletes. Initially, I thought this would be an easy task. It definitely wasn't! I'd often get frustrated when athletes didn't get my message, or think, "I keep telling them what to do, why aren't they getting it!" This method was a recipe in futility. The Persistent teacher/coach isn't about telling them what to do. It's much more about inspiring students, and making sure they know you care.

One other important point: developing the habit of being persistent sounds much easier than it actually is. As the year progresses, especially at the high school level, you will have students who may become lazy. I mean, what 12th-grade student wants to be in class with a week to go before graduation? I know that I was counting down the days once New Year's Day passed! This is why being persistent is not only important, but required. Here are an easy 3 to get started with:

1. Begin early in the year. Be clear from the beginning what you expect from every student. There will be those that test you, and if you're not absolutely steadfast with the guidelines for class, you'll just end up changing things frequently and confusing students. When I say begin early, I'm simply stating the importance of communicating your high expectations right away.
2. Model the benefits of the great work that students complete on time. Showing excellence from their peers is one of the best ways to inspire kids to improve on habits that they may not already have.

Also, the pride factor can never be overestimated. When you promote outstanding achievements from your students, it has a dramatic carry over influence on other kids in the class.
3. Be clear from the beginning that you truly care about the well-being of students. I've had persistent teachers who went about things with the wrong mindset. Screaming and punishing a student for not turning in work, or not paying attention, may seem like persistence. In my mind, that's poor classroom management and an even worse attitude.
Telling students why you're reminding them of things is about you wanting them to be successful. It's amazing the difference it will make when you say, "Listen, I'm sorry for bringing this up frequently, but your success is the most important thing in this class!"

After reading the 3Ps, it's time to focus on the 3E's that will help shape your class and school. Again, these three are not all-inclusive. Just as you could find other "P" words that are important, the same holds true for this section. I've focused on these words because they are part of the backbone of great teachers.

1st E - Empathy

> Empathy - the ability to understand and share the feelings of another (Barth, 2018).

No matter the grade level or gender, there will be instances where our students have difficulty both in school and in their personal lives. Sometimes things will go smoothly for an extended period of time, and you'll just sail along undeniably proud of the progress and fun your students are having. But then all of a sudden, with no warning, the "empathy piece" will become the difference maker for you and your class.

I remember when a few years ago my dog Izzy, a 16-year-old Golden Retriever, passed away. Coming into school that day was challenging to say the least. As a person who tries to maintain a positive attitude, my class could sense that something was off. After a few minutes, I mentioned that my dog had passed and how tough it was losing an amazing animal. Students could obviously see that my sorrow wasn't because I was mad at them, but rather from outside forces. Because our class had been built around a strong, positive, class community, many of the students were empathetic to my story and told their own stories about the loss of a pet. It helped me to always remember that young adults were able to see things from their teacher's perspective. We must do the same things for our students. Again, empathy isn't a one and done emotion that just comes and goes as the year passes. With many issues in the lives of our students, we'll need to consistently show how much we care about their well-being. Below are 3 tips that can help keep us focused on building empathy in class.

1. Students have lives outside of our actual class. It's so easy to get wrapped up in our own content and room, that we forget about all the other distractions, hobbies, work, family issues, etc.... that may occur on a daily basis. Being able to understand our students' lives is paramount to seeing the power of empathy in school.
2. Model what empathy looks like. No matter the grade level, many students won't know what the word means. Some might think of sympathy, but the difference, of course, is huge. Telling a personal story, giving examples or even just defining the word and having a discussion are key factors in helping students to understand that you promote an "empathetic classroom."
3. Reflection of our practice can be a powerful driver in how we teach and what students get out of our class. There will be times where you might not feel the need to show empathy.

We've all been there! I can recall a situation when I was on my prep period. I heard a boy screaming down the hall. As I walked down, he was yelling in an empty classroom, standing next to another one or one teacher. To make sure things were okay, I entered the room and sat down at my desk, just to make sure nothing escalated. Over the next 5-10 minutes, I witnessed the teacher demonstrate resolve and empathy towards this student that I've never witnessed during my long career. In each moment, you could see that she was reflecting on her actions and words to best meet the needs of this boy in need. By showing empathy, she not only totally diffused a volatile situation, but she also showed the young man and me how acts of kindness can be the difference in the lives of each of us.

2nd E - Empowering

> Empower: to make (someone) stronger and more confident, especially in controlling their life and claiming their rights (Pearsall, 1998).

I love the above definition! For me, it totally exemplifies what I'd want students to be when they are in my class, and more importantly when they leave it. You'd be hard pressed to find a teacher who wouldn't be happy with any student who is more confident and better able to make choices when they leave a class. Great schools help develop a mindset in their students that focuses on lasting learning beyond just the school walls. Being able to empower students, especially if done consistently, is transformational in nature.

I wish I could say that empowering students is easy. Unfortunately, at least for most educators, it isn't. Because of our current system of education, helping students to find their passion, become risk takers and develop true thinking skills, is much more difficult than it should be. We are used to telling students what to do, how long something should be, how many points it's worth, etc.... That will rarely inspire any student to do more than what's the minimum necessary. With that said, I'm hopeful that the suggestions below can at least guide you in the right direction. They are easy to implement and will allow you to build upon the steps that students take as the year progresses.

1. Start slowly. When I first really got involved in getting students empowered, my natural personality led me to jump full bore into making it work. Huge mistake!! Students need time to adjust to the totally different style of instruction and learning that you'll be asking them to master.

By easing the class into assignments that are easy to follow, clearly defined and exciting to work on, you'll save yourself the headaches of late work, huge variations in the quality and most importantly, you'll have students who will embrace taking bigger steps next time.

2. Explain why "empowering" them is important. I recall about 6 years ago, we had just finished a quiz. Students had a few minutes to reflect on what they wanted to accomplish going forward.

One student mentioned, "I want to be a better person!" That struck me to the core. We'd talked about being empowered before, but his words and actions going forward were more than just that "ahh" factor that many teachers think about when empowerment comes up. He understood that while learning the content was important, his purpose in class and school went far beyond just a test, quiz or project.

Also, you don't have to spend hours on this topic. Practice and modeling what empowering looks like can make a world of difference.
3. Have a goal in mind! Again, when I first started working on this change in instruction, it was all about giving kids options to help them love learning.

While I believe that is truly valuable, you must have clearer goals in mind when starting. For example, you might say, "Our goal is to create a short video presentation on a topic of your choice. It should be between 2-3 minutes and list why you chose it, how it's important to you and where you'd like to go next." That's vastly different than saying, "I want you to find a topic that interests you, design a project that shows you understand what you've learned, and present to class." The latter might work once students have figured things out, but if that's the initial step, you'll constantly be backtracking to explain the finer points and time will be wasted.

Empowering our students isn't just some fun, new, flash in the pan idea. Because of the advancements in technology, we must stress and impress upon our children the importance of learning because it's exciting. Many of the projects that were completed in my class would never have been done if I'd stuck with the typical teacher-led instruction. While things weren't always easy, the students benefited far more by exploring different avenues of learning, than by me presenting them with all the material. Give it a try! I'm sure you and your class will love the results.

3rd E - Enthusiasm

> Enthusiasm - intense and eager enjoyment, interest, or approval. (Oxford Dictionaries, n.d.)

Out of all the Ps and Es, enthusiasm is the easiest to understand from a teacher and student perspective. I hate making absolute statements, but in this case, here it goes: any teacher who shows a high level of enthusiasm is one who likes/loves their job, who is admired/loved by students, and who wants to make a difference each day. When you see that teacher in action, it's obvious that their enthusiasm shows how much they love teaching! They want to make the class exciting, fun and a place where every student enjoys coming to class. Educators who have high levels of enthusiasm usually show the other characteristics that were listed above. It's hard to imagine a teacher who is enthusiastic not having the traits of being: passionate, patient, persistent, empowering and empathetic. Sure, it's possible that some traits are more visible than others, but enthusiasm for teaching and learning is necessary for every class, and in every school. While enthusiasm is usually easy to see and often mentioned as a prerequisite for quality teaching, it's also something that can be developed with a few little mind games.

1. Fake it to make it. I know that others may disagree with this, but acting enthusiastic can really help change the temperament of a person. When others see your enthusiasm, and they show appreciation and happiness because of your enthusiastic nature, it becomes contagious. Everyone loves feeling good around a happy person, and that translates to the person bringing the happiness. After a while, if your consistent, you won't have to fake being enthusiasm, you actually will be!
Now I'm not suggesting that faking it every day will work. Rather, it's on those really tough days, that you aren't feeling it; that's when this little trick can work.

2. Stand at the door of your room.
Very few things will force the enthusiasm curve like greeting students as they enter. Just by being at the door is code for "good morning, hello, how are you, etc...."

These phases of acknowledgment, while small in nature help set the class up for an enthusiastic lesson and teacher.
3. Begin each lesson or class with something positive. Along the same lines as greeting students at the door, creating an initial positive reaction from students will definitely carry over to your lesson.

Teachers want students to love their class. They want children to come in smiling and feeling a part of a community. Positivity is a great builder of this.

After reading the 3Ps and 3Es, I'm hopeful that you at least reflect on how important they are for your career in education. As I've highlighted throughout the chapter, each of the six are skills that can be developed. To highlight:

- It is totally possible to grow a passionate attitude about your job.

- Becoming patient isn't just about teaching, it's also about personal life. Once you see improvement in one area, it leads to growth in the other.

- While persistence may seem tough, it's one of the best ways to manage classroom interactions and also show students you won't give up on them. Just by sticking with it, the difference will be huge.

- Great teachers share their lives with students. They want children to know who they are and what life experiences they've had. Empathy is a byproduct of that type of teaching. When you share your life with kids, they will share back!

- Nothing is more rewarding than watching students work diligently on something they love. Just as we have passions for our content, empowering students can lead to that same love of learning. Think about how many students become teachers! Part of that reason is that some teacher empowered them to seek greatness. That can be you!

- Finally, enthusiasm is all about attitude. Your ability to smile, laugh, be real and connect with kids makes all the difference. You'll feel great, and students will be the recipient when enthusiasm rules your class.

Thank you for taking the time to read the 3Ps and 3Es. Please connect with me on twitter at @Shapiro_WTHS #teachpos, Facebook or LinkedIn. Wishing you the very best on an amazing school year!

-Craig

References

Barth, F. D. (2018). Can empathy be taught? Retrieved from https://www.psychologytoday.com/us/blog/the-couch/201810/can-empathy-be-taught.

Oxford Dictionaries. (n.d.). Enthusiasm. Retrieved November 23, 2018, from https://en.oxforddictionaries.com/definition/enthusiasm

Pearsall, J., & Hanks, P. (Eds.). (1998). *The new Oxford dictionary of English*. Clarendon Press.

Vocabulary.com. (n.d.). Persistence. Retrieved November 23, 2018, from https://www.vocabulary.com/dictionary/persistence

EDUMATCH® SNAPSHOT IN EDUCATION (2018)

About the Author

Craig Shapiro

Craig Shapiro is a Health and Physical Education teacher at William Tennent High School in Warminster, Pennsylvania. Craig is a leading educator in the area of exercise, wellness and technology in the classroom, with a passion for developing relationship centered classrooms and schools. Craig has worked at the elementary, middle school and high school levels as a teacher and coach and has led numerous initiatives and programs to promote a "growth mindset."

Craig is the author of the upcoming book, Dream Big: Simple Steps to Transforming your Classroom. Craig has presented on Technology in the Classroom, Hooked on Health and Positive Climate in Schools. Craig believes that schools and classrooms should be student-centered and built around relationships. Craig is married with two teens and dogs Boomer and Bella! You can connect with Craig on his blog - CMSDreambig.com, Twitter @Shapiro_WTHS, and email boomerizzy@gmail.com.

Throwing Rocks into the Soul

Martine Brown

16-year-old Frederick Douglass becomes the catalyst of creating hope in my students.

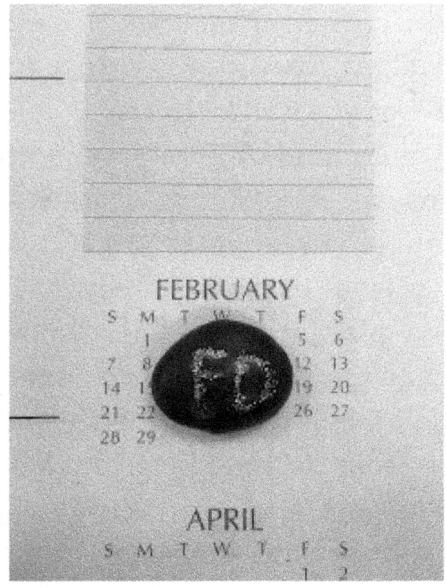

Every year I gave my students a rock, and they loved it. There is nothing

Martine Brown: Throwing Rocks into the Soul

special about this rock; it is black, hard, and virtually insignificant. For the students in room 2263, the rock became a symbol of courage, strength, and hope. Any time I run into a former student in the local grocery store or have one of my kiddos stop by my classroom, they let me know that have not forgotten and that they still have the rock; even though their initials have worn away.

My grade level team at the time decided to teach Frederick Douglass's autobiography, *Narrative of the Life of Frederick Douglass, An American Slave*. I read the story and fell in love with the connections to overcoming obstacles and determination. In chapter 10, Frederick Douglass was a 16-year-old boy who was leased to a plantation by his owner, Mr. Auld. He had never worked on a plantation and was immediately met with violence and abuse from as the slave breaker, Mr. Covey, who set out to tear away at Douglass's hope and sense of humanity. Frederick began to see a dark change in himself, and after one of Mr. Covey's beatings, Douglass returned bloodied and broken to his master to seek refuge. Mr.

Auld denied Douglass this, and sent him back to the plantation.

As Douglas stood in the woods, he considered taking his own life instead of returning. That is until he met Sandy, another slave who invited Douglass to stay for the night. During this meeting, Sandy gives Douglass a special root, and he is told to put on his right side to protect when he returns to the plantation. He told him that as long as he carried the root, he would never be beaten again. Now, to be honest, Douglass was not superstitious, but recognized that it couldn't hurt even if it didn't help. When Douglass returned to the plantation, Mr. Covey was prepared to give Douglass the lashing of his young life. However, Douglass fought back, in a way that he never had before. As a result of this battle, wrestling with his destiny in bondage was the foundation of the man that he would become, an iconic American abolitionist, speaker, and writer.

Frederick Douglass was no different than many of my students. He faced injustice, was neglected, unsure of himself and his purpose in the world. His family was torn apart, education was actively denied, and he did not know if he wanted to press on from day to day. He was, by the nature of the world lived in, a rock in a storm. Frederick Douglas had endured great hardships and to become an iconic American figure.

As I shared my excitement for the piece with one of my colleagues, it occurred to me I could be the "Sandy" in the lives of my students and give them a small gift that would encourage them to reach for the stars despite the roadblocks they may face. I thought of a seashell, but found it to be impractical. Maybe a diamond, not the real deal of course, but I knew this would not go over well with my boys. Finally, I came upon a rock and found it to be exactly what I was looking for. Every rock was as unique as my students, and I wrote their initials on each on to acknowledge their presence not just in my class, but in the world.

As my students' sneakers clamored into the room each year, they carry the baggage of destroyed families and generational curses. Secrets carry the tone of silence, the sound of hunger, poverty, negative stereotypes and racial disparities. Just like our kids, there are many things

Frederick Douglass could not control, but what he could control was his mind. I use this lesson to inspire my students to sharpen their minds, be like a rock in stormy weather, and conquer the obstacles outside of their control to achieve success. I think that the story of Frederick Douglass at 16 years old is a lesson that affects my students academically and personally because this narrative exemplifies the power of perseverance.

Instructional Strategies

Thinking about teaching the *Narrative of the Life of Frederick Douglass, An American Slave*? Here is a list of activities to support the text.

Annotate the text

Frederick Douglass uses rich language and complex sentences. As Frederick describes his experience, students mark the text for vocabulary, sentence variety, purpose, and theme. Since the new SAT test includes historical documents, this selection supports student learning.

Working collaboratively

Students work in small groups to analyze portions of the text. Each group presents their section of the text focusing on their analysis of what they read. The rest of the class takes notes during the presentations and read along.

Socratic Seminars

Is knowledge power? Students participate in a Socratic seminar to discuss major themes from the selection, the concept of being mentally free vs. physically free, for example. The outer circle can participate in a backchannel using Google Classroom. Backchannels allow students to discuss the major points of the seminar, cheer on fellow classmates, and offer additional support. Students are asked to analyze and defend their opinions using historical and literary text. This lesson helps students develop their written and speaking skills which support test-based writing.

Social media

Students can discuss what we can learn from Douglass as it relates to perseverance and their own lives. They will tweet and discuss any main ideas that they connected with. (140 characters or less, digitally or as an exit ticket).

Building relationships

The teacher tells the students that they will serve as a mentor; their support when the faced with adversity. Give each student a black rock (something symbolic) with their initials written in gold or silver permanent marker. Share with them that much like the selection, they will face moments that are as dark and hard as the rock. Remind students that they too can beat the odds, no matter how difficult it may seem. Close the discussion by emphasizing that education, learning, and moving forward in one's life are key to making dreams a reality.

About the Author

Martine Brown

Martine (MAR-TEEN) Brown is the Ready 1:1 Instructional Coach for Garland Independent School District. With 14 years of experience in education, Martine has worked with students as an English Language Arts and AVID Elective Teacher. In her current role as an instructional coach, she provides school and district level professional development, job-embedded support for effective strategies of 21st-century learning, and models effective instructional and digital strategies with teachers. In her free time, she enjoys running and participating in 5k races. In

2016, she ran her first 1/2 marathon. She also likes to style hair, cook, dance, spend quality time with her husband Kevin, and children Devin, Maxwell, and Charlotte. Her mantra is *Every Student Counts*, and it is her mission to be a catalyst of change in education.

Power of Being a Connected Educator

Rachelle Dene Poth

Why educators need to connect and how to become connected today

Education and the teaching profession have changed so much over the past 22 years that I have been in my classroom. There are so many demands on educators today, making it sometimes challenging to find time to connect with colleagues during the school day (or even outside of the school day). As educators, we are committed to lifelong learning and modeling this for our students. To do this means engaging in professional development that will push us to continue to develop our skills, so we are able to provide the best instruction for our students. With so many resources available to educators, learning and connecting are no longer confined to the physical interactions that occur within the classroom, school, or community. We have the opportunity to learn anywhere and at any time — we just need to be active in taking those first steps. It is important to work toward expanding our learning community and connecting with others. This holds true for our students and especially for educators.

Years ago, I was amazed at how often I would leave school and not have even had the chance to talk to my neighboring teachers. Teaching in a small school, it is surprising that we can go days without seeing people who teach right down the hall or even right across from us. Brief interactions did not even happen within the school, let alone finding time to meet outside of the classroom or after the school day.

Fortunately, becoming a more connected educator has never been easier, and the benefits extend beyond the teacher, to the students in the classroom as well. When we connect with other educators, we learn new tools, strategies, and ideas, which can inspire teachers to do more and spread the passion for learning to students, too.

My PLN

For years, I did not really have a PLN (Professional Learning Network). I had work friends and other colleagues that I knew I could count on, but our connections really ended at the end of the school day. Aside from email, we did not really communicate too much outside of school. I don't recall that there was any type of technology or as much of a focus on the different social media platforms and tools for connecting as there are today and that continue to develop each year. I was doing just fine on my own, or so I thought, because I didn't know anything different. My support system existed at school and through some friends who were working in various educational positions in nearby school districts.

So why do you need a PLN?

There are many benefits to being part of a PLN (Personal or Professionale

Learning Network), but I think the biggest is having access to a constant system of support. Depending on how you make those connections, you can connect with anyone in the world at any time. Thinking back to five years ago, before I became more connected, I can recall trying to find resources or ways to reach out to other educators when I had questions. This was quite time-consuming and centered around looking things up on the Internet, searching through books that I had purchased, or simply creating everything new or repurposing older materials. Once I became a part of a PLN, I spent less time accessing new ideas, learning about digital tools, brainstorming teaching methods by relying on my former searching tactics, and instead had more time and relied heavily on my PLN. The extra time enabled me to focus on changing my instruction, on finding more ways to spend time working with my students, and being able to provide diverse learning experiences in my classroom.

Beyond the access to tangible resources for instruction, being "connected" means having a personal and professional support system available whenever you need it and wherever you are. There are always times that we can plan to connect in person whether it be with our own colleagues or during local conferences, but this still proves to be difficult because of the lack of time or based on our respective locations. So, what is the solution to this ongoing problem of not having enough time? Technology. We can connect virtually through the different forms of social media and web tools that promote anytime and anywhere collaborating, communicating and conferencing. The question then becomes which tool to use, which one will serve your needs the best.

  In years past, we had to spend so much time looking for resources, searching through books and older course materials, or even traveling for professional development. The professional development that we choose needs to be more personalized to our needs and our interests. While there are of course times that all educators need to be a part of the same professional development sessions, in the same space, we now have many options that don't require us to leave our homes to participate in. (Although it is nice to get out and meet our PLN F2F). When it comes to our teaching practice or the tasks we have for our respective roles in education, we don't necessarily need to create all of our own materials or wait in line at the copier. (if we are in the habit of making packets, or relying on handouts for meeting agendas, but that is another conversation entirely). We have our network to reach out to for new ideas and learning opportunities.

How to Connect

Educators today have access to thousands of resources instantly, simply by connecting through our devices and reaching out into our "network." The power of connecting leads to collaborating, sharing our own ideas and gathering new ones, building on our strengths, and honing in on areas in which we need to grow. Through our PLN, we have these opportunities and whatever we need available to us at any time. We just need to decide how to connect, whether it be through Twitter, Facebook, Voxer or any of the learning communities out there.

Becoming Part of an Unexpected PLN

We can actively seek out different groups or form our own PLN. But there are also times that we just happen to become part of a PLN, or a PLF (Personal or Professional Learning Family). I have been part of several groups. I first became connected in 2014 after being selected as a Keystone Technology Innovator for Pennsylvania. I spent a week at a Technology Summit learning about all things educational and technology-related, where someone sent out a tweet and used what they thought was my Twitter handle. It was from that point on that I started to use Twitter, learn more about PLNs and the value of Twitter and other social media tools for connecting.

I remember when I first heard about the "power of a PLN," I just didn't get it. I thought it simply referred to a "colleague" or having "work friends" as they are often called, but just under a different name. I have learned that I was way off about my understanding of a PLN. I have become "connected" through several PLNs that have also somehow interconnected with one another. It has become a super PLN, or mega PLN. And it evolved through Social Media, which I was so wrong about the value of it for education. Sometimes we make these connections, develop relationships that grow into something powerful and life-changing, without even realizing it while it is happening.

I became a member of EduMatch during the summer of 2016, and I am amazed at the number of people that I have been able to connect with from around the world. What makes it even better is being able to meet for the first time face-to-face and have the feeling as though you've known one another for a really long time. You quickly learn who to reach out to for advice, who has certain experience in different areas of education, with different technology tools, pretty much anything. Sarah Thomas, the founder of EduMatch, has been amazing at creating a welcoming space for connecting educators from around the world, creating a real PLF (Professional and Personal Learning Family), with the goal of empowering ourselves so that we can empower others

My Core PLN

My first true PLN is now referred to as the "53s," a group that grew from a Facebook community made up of ISTE 2016 attendees, created by Rodney Turner (@techyturner), that then evolved into a Voxer group. Rodney's message was to make connections, that if we see someone sitting alone, we should ask them to join our group.

As a group, we met face-to-face at ISTE 2016 in Denver. There are also a few members of this core group that I met through Twitter chats and other conferences, and was fortunate to be able to spend time with them learning in the same physical space. We welcomed our other friends into the group and continued to build our core PLN. We have come together to be referred to as the 53s, a name which is significant to us. The name (#my53s) evolved after our initial core group outgrew its original acronym of "JMRR." Our group is based on trust, transparency, empathy, kindness, pushback, fun and passion for education and the power of learning, and most importantly, true friendship and constant support.

These people, my friends, are my source of inspiration and the ones that I rely on heavily each day. We are a unique group that spans the United States and Canada. I am so fortunate to be a part of a core PLN that I know will be there for me no matter what. The only thing I wish I could change about our group is our geographical locations. We are from different states and a different country, and so time together does not happen that often. But when it does, it truly is the best time ever. We push one another to take some risks, to step out of our comfort zone and try new things, to dare to enter into a Snapchat #singoff, to create #BookSnaps, and to bust out with #carpoolkaraoke. We have had amazing times together at FETC, USM Summer Spark, ShiftinEDU and ISTE and there are more to come!

I am not sure where I would be without my 53s. The times we have shared are so special, and I am so thankful for this group and wish for everyone to have a core PLN like this: Evan Abramson, Jarod Bormann, Jennifer Casa-Todd, Jaime Donally, Mandy Froehlich, Tisha Richmond, and Rodney Turner. Our group expanded to include our awesome Snapchat singing group which includes the 8 of us, and also Tara Martin, Andrew Easton, and Mandy Taylor. They are an amazing group of educators, who would drop everything to be there to support you. I am proud and honored to call them my friends.

Connecting through Voxer: Another PLN and PLF

I am also fortunate to be connected with two other tremendous groups (my PLF) and cannot wait to meet more of them in person. The #4OCFPLN and Edugladiators!

I have followed the Edugladiators and connected with the "Core Warriors" during their Saturday morning chats for a few years. Always inspired by their conversation and the positive messages shared by the group, I looked forward to being involved each weekend, making new connections for my PLN. I was honored when asked by Marlena Gross Taylor, to become one of the Core Warriors, and help to spread the word about change, empowerment, and advocacy in education. Being able to meet with several of the other Core Warriors has been a tremendous experience, and they are more than just educators, they have become mentors and more importantly friends.

Rachelle Dene Poth: Power of Being a Connected Educator

EDUMATCH® SNAPSHOT IN EDUCATION (2018)

Rachelle Dene Poth: Power of Being a Connected Educator

#Allthethings

PLN with a hashtag, website, stickers, shirts, and bracelets!

I had read the book "Four O'Clock Faculty" by Rich Czyz and joined in the Voxer book study for it earlier this year. Once the book study ended, many members of the group stayed connected and kept the conversation going. A group of educators from around the country, with different backgrounds, experiences, and roles in education, collectively decided to keep the group together to connect and grow long after the book study had ended. We have become a real PLF (the #4OCFPLN). I have enjoyed learning new things from this group every day and knowing that they are there when I need them.

There are so many great conversations, a lot of laughs and fun that happens within this group every day. I love knowing that I can reach out to this group at any time. It is a very supportive and passionate group of educators with a lot of diverse perspectives and a bond that continues to grow and get stronger and better each day. Laughs, inside jokes, challenges, pushback, inspiration and amazing connections. REAL connections. We know more about each other and learn and push boundaries of learning every day. This is exactly what it means to be connected and to be a part of a PLN. The only true way to understand the power of a PLN is to experience it for yourself. Get connected today!

Where to Begin

Everybody needs to be part of a PLN. Not only does it benefit you as an educator, more importantly, but it also leads to greater opportunities for our students. Depending on your time and what you're looking for, there are so many different options available for making these connections fit with your schedule and based on your interests. It might be formed through Twitter, and it might be through a book study or other focus group using Voxer, or one of the other social media tools out there. A list to choose from includes becoming a member of EduMatch, joining ISTE or connecting with others using Slack, Facebook, or some of the different edtech organizations and tech company ambassador programs. It doesn't really matter what you use, as long as you take time to make connections that will help you to continue to grow and have the support you need when you need it. Whether it is a group you join, a chat you follow, or a mix, get out there and connect. The best is when we get to spend time together, learn from each other, share the same nervousness before giving an ignite, and knowing that there is always someone there to help you whenever you need.

How to get started connecting today

1. Join a PLN. Just making the decision to join a Personal or Professional Learning Network (PLN) is a great first step to take. Connected educators rely on their PLN (often referred to as one's "tribe") to ask questions, share resources, offer support and be supported. And sometimes even to debate, pushback, and challenge one another to work harder and keep growing. It is a reliable and reassuring way to gather feedback, especially when trying new things or taking some risks. You don't have to do it alone.

   Start tweeting. If you don't already have a Twitter account as an educator, then I recommend definitely creating one. Even though I was so against Twitter years ago, I admit how wrong I was about it.

Knowing what I do now, I recommend that you create your account, begin searching for people you know or recognize in education and follow them (most will follow you back and help grow your follower numbers) and then find an education chat or hashtag to explore. And once you do, tag me in a tweet using @Rdene915.

Chats: You can find chats occurring every day of the week, all hours of the day, which are focused on a variety of education topics, and specific to different roles in education (i.e., teachers, administrators, tech coaches). You don't have to start with everything at once; just set aside a few minutes each day, a few days a week, to see what the chat is about and to make more connections.

Trying something new can be scary. If you're not sure where to start with Twitter, ask a few of your colleagues if they use Twitter and which chats they follow. Another option is to simply use Google to search "Twitter chats," which will lead you to many great websites listing resources to help you get started. Two of my favorites are Cybraryman (Jerry Blumengarten @cybraryman1). Check out his page for a list of chats, hashtags, and a schedule to find something that meets an area of interest. I also highly recommend Participate, for a list of chats, topics, and ease of getting involved in the conversations.

Hashtags: You can't go wrong simply by following #education, #edchat, #edtechchat, #teaching and/or #students (just to name a few). Just type the hashtag into the search function on Twitter, and you can view the latest Tweets discussing that topic. There are even lists curated by various websites, including Getting Smart and Global Citizen.

If you want to quickly experience the benefits of being connected through Twitter, ask a question and include one or more of the popular hashtags in your tweet, and see how quickly people respond and the new "followers" you have. The more invested you get with Twitter, you may look into Tweetdeck or Hootsuite for managing multiple chats and scheduling tweets.

2. Resources. There are also blogs and books you can check out today that focus on helping educators become more connected. One book I recommend is "What Connected Educators Do Differently" by Todd Whitaker, Jeffrey Zoul and Jimmy Casas, which offers great insight into the reasons for

becoming connected and how to get started.

Connecting tomorrow

1. **Online Communication.** The best part about Twitter is that it promotes global connections that can lead to other opportunities for communicating and building your PLN. Some options are Voxer, a walkie-talkie messaging tool that enables live conversation and the ability to instantly share resources, images, GIFS, videos and more. There are groups created specifically to certain themes, it can be a great space for running a book study, Twitter chat groups and even smaller discussion groups. It can be used with educators in your building, with students for reflections, or PBL as I have used it for, and even for simply recording your own ideas and reflections under "My notes." Voxer is free and also has a PRO version which offers more options and is not too costly. Some PLNs have created a communication channel using Slack for more streamlined conversations.

These are all great tools for facilitating connections with other educators and to enable students to connect easily with other students, simply by sending a Vox and asking for someone to talk with your class.

2. **Join an edcamp.** There are many organizations offering classes and edcamps throughout the country and world nearly every Saturday. Edcamps are opportunities to access free, authentic PD, meet other educators, experience an "unconference" and help to create the "schedule" for the day, surrounded by diverse people and perspectives. The great thing about Edcamps is that the topics are based on the interests of those present, making it more personalized. But even better than that, it's another opportunity to establish connections made through Twitter, add to your PLN and meet with other educators and nearby schools to expand your learning circle.

Connections to plan for

1. **Attend conferences.** Look for local and national conferences, which are fantastic opportunities once you have connected on Twitter or through Voxer, to meet face-to-face with members of your newfound PLN.

There are many conferences you can attend based on current hot topics, your personal interests or even areas that you'd like to explore. Talk to members of your PLN to find out what conferences they attend, and make plans to get to one together. Personally, FETC, ISTE, PETE&C, and USM Summer Spark have created the most opportunities for me to meet F2F with members of my PLNs.

2. **Organizations and EdTech Ambassador Programs.** While attending or preparing to attend conferences or by simply searching online, take some time to explore the different memberships available through education-focused organizations. Here are a few recommendations:

I recommend becoming a member of the EduMatch Community. It is so full of events for learning and growing, with a Voxer group, publishing company, Twitter chats and panel discussions, and other opportunities for really building your PLN.

Another possibility is joining the International Society for Technology in Education (ISTE) or one of its state affiliates. There are online Professional Learning Communities which offer opportunities such as webinars, Twitter Chats, book studies, and online discussion communities which promote interaction and networking, and opens up many doors to educators and learning experiences around the world.

You can also consider becoming an ambassador through educator programs such as Common Sense Education, Google Certified Educators, Microsoft Innovative Educators, or any of the many edtech companies that have programs available. I enjoy being a Nearpod PioNear. These communities also plan events focused on networking and ways to promote new learning experiences.

Why Create/Join a PLN?

Becoming part of a PLN will help you to continue to learn, grow, and thrive as an educator. It will open up a world of learning opportunities for you, but more importantly for your classroom and your learning community. Imagine the possibilities available from being able to instantly have a conversation with an educator around the world who can talk to your students about the topic of the day, without doing anything more than opening the app on your phone and talking.

Conversations and growth through these connections will enable us to transform our thinking, broaden our perspectives, and not feel isolated and alone in our roles as educators. If we want to transform student learning, we have to first think about bettering ourselves. We are better together, so get connected today. Start by connecting with me on Twitter or Voxer, @rdene915.

References

Whitaker, Todd. Zoul, Jeffrey. Casas, Jimmy (2015). What Connected Educators Do Differently, Routledge, First Edition

About the Author

Rachelle Dene Poth

Rachelle Dene Poth is a Spanish and STEAM: What's nExT in Emerging Technology Teacher at Riverview Junior-Senior High School in Oakmont, PA. She is also an attorney and earned her Juris Doctor Degree from Duquesne University of Law in 2006, and has a Master's Degree in Instructional Technology. She has presented at conferences such as ISTE,

FETC, iNACOL, PETE&C, PSMLA, ShiftinEDU, Summer Spark and additional local conferences, on technology and more ways to benefit student learning. She is the President of the ISTE Teacher Education Network and the Communications Chair of the ISTE Mobile Learning Network.

Rachelle received the gold Presidential Award for service to education by completing more than 500 hours in her work with ISTE. She was selected as the 2017 Outstanding Teacher of the Year by PAECT (the Pennsylvania Association for Educational Communications in Technology, the PA affiliate of ISTE) and by the NSBA as one of the "20 to watch" educators for 2017.

She is connected in several communities including being an Ambassador Buncee, CoSpaces, Flipgrid, and an Edmodo Certified Trainer, Nearpod PioNear, and TES Ambassador. Rachelle is a Microsoft Innovative Educator Expert and is Google Certified Levels I and II.

She enjoys writing and has been blogging for four years. She has recently authored a few chapters in the 2016 and 2017 editions of the EduMatch books.

Rachelle is a contributing author to "Gamify Literacy" from ISTE and the IGI Global Publication of Social Presence, with a chapter on building an online presence for learning. She also blogs regularly for DefinedSTEM, Getting Smart and Kidblog. Her areas of expertise include blended learning, project-based learning, digital tools for assessments, and Augmented and virtual reality.

Rachelle is currently working on three books which are due out early in 2019. The first will be a part of the new "UN" series from Times 10 Publishing, called uNconventional." She is also publishing with EduMatch and Edugladiators.

Preparing to Lead: Coaching for Aspiring and Novice School Leaders

Sharon H. Porter, Ed.D.

Preparing assistant principals for the principalship.

Introduction

I have had the opportunity to coordinate my school district's induction program for assistant principals since the inception of the program. This is year five that I have been working with first- and second-year assistant principals and principals. While the job description of an assistant principal is quite similar from state to state and school districts across the country, the roles and responsibilities of assistant principals vary even within school districts.

This chapter will discuss the need for school districts to assist in the preparation and development of its school leaders. Coaching, mentoring, and job-embedded development will be the focus.

The Importance of Coaching Novice Leaders

There are several players involved as it relates to developing school leaders. University school leadership programs, the novice leader themselves, the school district as a whole, as well as the supervising principal. University school leadership programs generally play the initial role in formal leadership development. Numerous studies indicate a change in university principal preparation programs is needed. In my recent research for my dissertation, university principal preparation program research was reviewed. However, my focus was on the local education agency (LEA). You may wonder why, but I look at my own experience. I received my administrator certification in 2000. While I was appointed an assistant principal shortly thereafter (2001), I did not become a principal until 2007. So many things had changed during that time.

Coaching and mentoring absolutely must be a part of a school district's plan in placing leaders in schools. Coaching should be meaningful, relevant, and should support the development of the novice leaders. Coaching often times must be conducted by evaluators or supervisors of the coachee. Those roles vary in major ways. Authority and power are key components of evaluators and supervisors. Confidentiality also should play a major role in coaching.

Carol Dweck's along with Lisa Blackwell and colleagues at Stanford University's research on achievement and success revealed the significance of two mindsets; Growth and Fixed. A growth mindset should be the basis of school leadership coaching. As a leadership coach for novice leaders, I emphasize how challenges and barriers are inevitable, but should always be seen as an opportunity to learn and grow. The coaching relationship should be transformational. When the appropriate tools are utilized, and effected skills and strategies are implemented, growth and development are supported.

I also believe that preparation should not begin with the appointment of the job of an administrator. As a teacher, individuals should be afforded opportunities to lead in preparation of the assistant principalship as well as assistant principals having full school leadership experience before the appointment as principal. Both experiences will depend on the initiative of the individual as well as the will and/or skill of the principal.

The 2007 Wallace report, *Preparing School Leaders for a Changing World,* contended that well-prepared principals make a significant difference in their schools. What is important to note about that study is the emphasis on preparedness. The study focuses on how school leaders were prepared before becoming school principals for the principalship. You can be well-prepared if systems and structures are in place to allow that preparation. Coaching is focused on the development of specific skills. There must be ongoing self-reflection, quality feedback, and intentional dialogue with the school leader.

In *Leverage Leadership* (Bambrick-Santoya, 2012), six steps of effective feedback are identified as key action steps to avoid common myths of feedback. I follow each step during a coaching session.

Step 1: Precise praise. During my planning for the coaching session, I review my notes from the previous session as well as any observation notes I have from a prior visit. I always start the coaching session with "precise praise."

Step 2: Probe. Probing is also part of my Preparation Phase. I prepare targeted open-ended questions about the topics we are discussing.

Step 3: Identify the problem and concrete action steps. This step is implemented during the coaching session in collaboration with the school leader. The questions are designed to allow the school leader to identify the problem and the necessary action steps.

Step 4: Practice. Practice is where the thought partnership comes alive. This allows the school leader to have an opportunity to feel, see and hear what an action may look, sound, or feel like prior to revealing to the staff or leadership team.

Step 5: Plan ahead. While we "practice" we also begin "planning ahead." Next steps are identified which leads to...

Step 6: Set a timeline. Setting a timeline for implementation is a key component to ensuring implementation.

As a leadership development coach, I see myself as a thought partner for the novice leader, asking the thought-provoking questions that will allow the leader to arrive at their own answers. I had the opportunity to participate in training at the Center for Creative Leadership (CCL, n.d.) in North Carolina. Their six core principles for coaching are:

1. Create a Safe Environment
2. Keep the Principal in Charge
3. Facilitate and Collaborate
4. Advocate Self-Awareness
5. Promote Experiential Learning
6. Model What You Coach

I live by these six core principles as a leadership development coach.

Coaching Competencies

What should coaches do before, during, and after a coaching session? This was my question when I became a leadership coach initially. The International Coach Federation (ICF) identifies 11 coach competencies that are divided into four specific categories: Setting the foundation, Co-creating the relationship, communicating effectively, and Facilitating learning and results. Now that I coach through my private coaching firm and also a school district, I have been able to implement research-based coaching competencies to support growth and development. Through my experience, I focus on the following four areas: Preparation, Relationship Building, Reflection, and Application.

During the **Preparation Phase**, I review the leader's goals and any data that is available. I also utilize a coaching agreement to outline the expectation of coaching sessions. I map out points of discussions and potential questions to facilitate the conversation. Open-ended questions are asked regarding instructional as well as management topics that generally stem from a follow-up from the previous meeting. When I am prepared, the coaching session is more meaningful and productive. The process of learning and implementing new knowledge is more evident.

Relationship Building is crucial to the coaching relationship. Many of the novice leaders in my professional coaching, I have prior professional relationships. But there are times when the novice leader and I do not have an established relationship. Building trust and allowing the leader to feel safe in the coaching space that I create is imperative. I focus on collaboration, quality, authentic feedback, support, and transparency.

Tschannen-Moran (2014) identifies the five facets of trust as Benevolence, Reliability, Competency, Honesty, and Openness. Each of the facets is extremely important to establish an effective coaching relationship

I am an advocate of self-reflection. While a client is **self-reflecting**, I must engage in active listening and copious note-taking. I am able to push their thinking as they self-reflect. Also, after each coaching session, I engage in self-reflection and utilize my written notes to identify areas that could use improvement as well as areas in the session that I was able to appropriately implement effective coaching skills such as listening, questioning, providing feedback, and assess my non-verbal communication.

The final phase of application is where the action lies. Goals are set and implemented, data is collected, and the client's progress is monitored.

School Leadership Redefined

No longer is school leadership defined in management terms. School leaders are now instructionally-focused, are change agents, and visionary leaders. Management responsibilities still exist and are an important part of leadership. There is, without doubt, a heavier focus on teaching and learning. Elmore (2004) noted, "if we do not focus on how students learn, then what is the point of our efforts to change schools?"

Effective school leaders must articulate a strong vision, clearly outlining the purpose and core values to all stakeholders, establishing and maintaining a positive school culture, and continuously assessing the needs of the students.

Effective school leadership is essential to increased student achievement and overall school improvement. Principal leadership is second only to classroom teachers (Leithwood, Louis, Anderson, & Wahlstrom, 2004). While the school leader cannot be a content expert in every curriculum, establishing a leadership team that shares that expertise is monumental. The school leader must be strategic and intentional when creating the leadership team. Marzano, Waters, and McNulty (2005) coin it as "crafting a purposeful community."

Conclusion

This chapter addressed the need for the intentional preparation of school leaders and the continuous coaching of novice school leaders. In order to strengthen the principal pipeline, school districts must invest in deliberate leadership development for both aspiring school leaders as well as novice leaders. School leaders' roles have shifted from those of managers to instructional leaders.

Effective school leaders monitor and evaluate the delivery of instruction, communicate effectively; demonstrate knowledge of curriculum, instruction, and assessment; engage the school community; establish relationships and positive school culture; as well as develop leadership capacity within their staff.

Leadership coaching is necessary in education. Hargrave (2008) noted that the purpose of having a coach is "to expand an individual's capacity to obtain desired results and to facilitate that individual's organizational development." Trust is considered to be the most essential component in successful coaching relationships.

References

Bambrick-Santoyo, Paul, 1972-. (2012). Leverage leadership: a practical guide to building exceptional schools. San Francisco: Jossey-Bass,

Center for Creative Leadership. (n.d.). The 6 essential principles of leadership coaching. Retrieved November 24, 2018, from https://www.ccl.org/multimedia/podcast/the-six-principles-of-leadership-coaching/

Elmore, R. (2004). School reform from the inside out. Cambridge, MA: Harvard University Press

Hargrove, R. (2008). Masterful coaching (3rd ed.) San Francisco, CA: Jossey-Bass.

International Coach Federation, (n.d.). *Core competencies*. Retrieved from https://coachfederation.org/core-competencies

Leithwood, K., Louis, K. S., Anderson, S. & Wahlstrom, K. (2004). How leadership influences student learning. Retrieved from https://www.wallacefoundation.org/knowledge-center/Documents/How-Leadership-Influences-Student-Learning.pdf

Marzano, R. J., Waters, T., & McNulty, B. A. (2006). *School leadership that works: From research to results.* Heatherton, Vic.: Hawker Brownlow Education.

About the Author

Sharon H. Porter, Ed.D.

Dr. Sharon H. Porter (Dr. Sharon) resides in the Washington, DC area. She is owner of Perfect Time SHP LLC, Coaching, Consulting, and Book Publishing Firm, Founder of the G.R.I.N.D. Entrepreneur Network™, Host of the I Am Dr. Sharon ™ Show, Creator and Host of Write the Book Now!™, Leadership Matters with Dr. Sharon™, and The GRIND Entrepreneur Network Spotlight Podcasts.

Dr. Sharon has served as an educator for over 25 years. She currently serves as a Leadership Development Coach for novice principals and assistant principals in a large urban school district in the Washington DC area. She is a former elementary and middle school principal. She earned a Bachelor of Science (B.S.) in Elementary Education at Winston-Salem State University, a Master of Education (M.Ed.) in Curriculum & Instruction at National-Louis University, Administration & Supervision Post Graduate Certification at the Johns Hopkins University, an Educational Specialist (Ed.S.) degree at Walden University, and a Doctorate of Education (Ed. D.) in Educational Leadership & Policy Studies from Howard University.

Dr. Sharon holds a National Association of Elementary School Principal (NAESP) Principal Mentor Certification, is a Gallup Certified Strengths Coach, an Official Member of Forbes Coaches Council and a member of the International Women Association.

Culturally Competent Teacher Recruitment and Retention

Rian Reed

Seeing every child thrive means starting with the teacher

The living breathing impact of diversity and inclusion for teachers and students can be found in the daily commitment of educational leaders like William Anderson at Manual High School in Denver who helps make innovative instructional practices transformational for school communities! (Reed, 2018) Mr. Anderson, a Black male educator, works through the Distributive Leadership Model to both instruct his students and empower the self-efficacy of educators. Yet, when we scan our nation, the National Center for Educational Statistics shows that only

6.8% of teachers in the U.S. are educators of color (Anderson, 2018).

This lack of diversity leads us to topics like Black Lives Matter being misunderstood and overlooked as viable topics for social-emotional and academic growth. In order to dispel bias in education for both the educator and students, more educators of color must be recruited and supported as they shape the lives of students and their community.

Dr. Tamara Dias, Executive Director of the African American Teaching Fellows (www.aatf.org), states that, "when students see themselves reflected in their teachers, it gives them a glimpse into all that is possible for them. Faculty diversification has the power to shatter historical stereotypes, and increasing diversity has the ability to transform school communities." So how do we recruit and retain educators like Mr. Anderson so that we can reach the level of impact described by Dr. Dias? Here are three areas of improvement that will cause systematic changes in how educators of color are recruited and retained.

Teaching Certification Support Systems

One place we can start is by building a support system around potential educators of color to finish their teaching certification. Deignton Boyd, who was recently featured on the NBC News segment on African-American teachers' impact in Philadelphia Schools, stated on Reminisce: The Empowered Podcast that he sees a roadblock in people of color not being able to pass the Teaching Certification exam. He notes that his peers in undergraduate programs turn to other professions so that they can still impact children, but not under the role of teacher.

Teaching certification supports are the solution to this roadblock. Programs like the Color of Teaching at Millersville University of Pennsylvania founded by Dr. Miriam Witmer, do just that. Not only do they encourage current students interested in becoming teachers through practicum and social-emotional support, but they also build relationships with High School students to guide them in the journey to seek out the role of educator as their current profession (Witmer, 2018). This initial engagement and coaching ensure that educators of color do not get stuck before the plane of their future takes off.

The programs provide social-emotional supports, as well as assists students of color in navigating being the "only person of color" in their education classes. Also, it provides support in navigating the ins and outs of the college experiences, which is particularly viable for first-generation college students. Programs like Color of Teaching essentially build community around the path to teaching mutually benefiting the individual and the teaching profession.

Onboarding Success

After educators of color obtain the needed credentials, there must be systems in place to ensure that they obtain employment and grow to increase their impact. In Charlottesville, Virginia, The African American Teaching Fellows (AATF) services its community in this way to shift the narrative by reducing the student drop-out through increased presence of educators that look like the students they teach. Features of onboarding support provided by AATF include "offering tuition scholarships, mentoring support, professional development, and a social network for our educators" (T. Dias, personal communication, July 29, 2018). This might include interview tips, how to set up a classroom, and improving instructional practices for students with a variety of needs such as Students with Special Needs and English Language Learners.

Dr. Dias also stresses the importance of creating an environment where educators are in a "safe space" where they can express their concerns without fear of repercussion, but one where their growth is encouraged. There are also well-known organizations like Teach for America; however, systems should also embed onboarding supports. Beyond typical new teacher professional development workshops, principals should include new teachers within the culture of the school from a daily logistics of how to navigate the grading and attendance system to school-wide traditions. There should be small support groups and individual mentors within the building to address immediate wonderings.

During these small group sessions, new teachers should be provided with a manual directly related to the ins and outs of the school. One of the key components of these small groups is active listening and follow through from the leadership. If there is a lack of authenticity in the application of ideas presented by the new teachers, it deteriorates trust. A lack of trust in the onboarding process prevents a strong foundation from being formed and isolates the teacher, which ultimately negatively impacts the student.

Voice Amplification through Leadership Roles

Principals should not shy away from enlisting new teachers for leadership opportunities, as a new teacher is not always synonymous with inexperience. To further support the growth of educators of color and the students that they teach, the voice of the educator of color must be amplified through leadership roles. Fresh, innovative ideas from a diverse leadership team lead to culturally competent perspectives that empower students of color, while also empowering the teacher leader of color as well. It is also important to note that diversity expands beyond physical appearance but to ability levels, gender identity and a variety of life experiences. This also includes the importance of hiring individuals who live in the neighbors in which the school resides to ensure that the educators understand the students' community celebrations and challenges. Through valuing and empowering the students, the diverse voices in the room who were a part of the decision-making also feel valued and empowered increasing the longevity of their tenure. Leadership will subsequently see a shift in the culture to community and academic growth for all students (Camera, 2018).

Making more strategic decisions related to how we engage teachers of color will subsequently support the growth of students. If our educational system ensures that pre-service teachers are supported differently in the teaching certification support systems, onboarding to a school system, and amplification of the voices of teachers of color through leadership roles, our schools and communities will indeed thrive.

A Reflection: Philosophy on Black Education

To be creative, to be innovative, to be empowered within our global community, persons of color can thrive and celebrate our greatest selves through education. The curricular academic path for the Black child can be found in the synopsis of the following 3 principles:

My physical appearance, agility, and wisdom are valuable.

The education of the Black child begins by cultivating an environment that values their core being. Where their innate creativity, caramelized shades, hair products, and textures can be freely expressed without being criminalized. Where their ideas around Science, Math, the Arts, Engineering, Technology, consciousness, Emotional Intelligence, and the fundamentals are affirmed through the key Black leaders that impacted these industries from the beginning of time.

I am a valuable member of my home, my community, and global spaces.

The education of the Black child is liberating to the mind, empowers the family, and catapults the sustainability of the community. The Black child is a part of a collective force that adds to the success of our ancestors. We speak multiple languages, travel, and apply the ideology of Sankofa as we grow as individuals; bringing back wisdom to impact economic development and social change across seas. It is the exposure, partnership and the affirming space that gives the Black child the opportunity to thrive.

I see myself in the vision of tomorrow.

The education of the Black child begins with the resources that they are exposed to. Do the books that they read, speakers that they hear, teachers that guide them, and leaders that empower them reflect their image? When this happens, the Black child can see themselves in the future. Their fears are only stepping stones as their motivation to thrive says, "keep going, you can do it, and you are almost there!" Their dreams are within reach because they see themselves succeeding in all experiences of life.

In all, these principles only begin the educational journey of the Black child, as the future is in found in their own hands, hearts, and minds — perfectly formed and perfectly created for our todays and our tomorrows!

References

Anderson, M. (2018). A Root Cause of the Teacher-Diversity Problem. Retrieved from https://www.theatlantic.com/education/archive/2018/01/a-root-cause-of-the-teacher-diversity-problem/551234/

Camera, Lauren. "States to Prioritize Hiring Teachers of Color." *U.S. News & World Report*, U.S. News & World Report, 28 Mar. 2018, www.usnews.com/news/education-news/articles/2018-03-28/states-to-prioritize-hiring-teachers-of-color.

Dias, T. (2018, 29 July). Personal interview.

Reed, R. (Producer and Host). (2018, July 22) Reminisce: The Empowered Podcast [Audio Podcast}. Retrieved from https://anchor.fm/reminisce/episodes/Episode-11-Black-Male-Educators-Building-Momentum-for-Impact-e1rind

Witmer, M. (2018). Color of Teaching. Retrieved from https://www.millersville.edu/edfoundations/coloroft/index.php

About the Author

Rian Reed

Rian Reed, MBA is an Educator Entrepreneur who is using the digital space to empower at the intersection of life and impact. With 7 years of teaching as a Special Educator in the K-12 system and over 12 years of leadership experience within the National Association for The Advancement of Colored People (NAACP) at the Local, State and National levels, her passion for civil rights and educational equality shape how she builds community. In March 2018, she presented at Harvard University on Colorblind Curriculums: Unwrapping Literacy and Numeracy in a Culturally Responsive Teaching and Learning Classroom sharing innovative strategies to build teacher capacity in their ability to apply culturally relevant teaching practices for student growth. In the digital space, she hosts Reminisce: The Empowered Podcast to amplify the truth in our collective voices that inspire change in all sectors of life. Her most recent podcast episode included in a panel of Black Male Educators from around the county to discuss why and how we can improve the statistics that there are only 2% of African-American Male teachers in the United States.

Miss Reed currently teaches English at a High School in Laurel, MD where she is actively involved in building community as the Freshman Class Sponsor, Assistant Softball Coach, and the go-to person all things Google Apps for Education. She is also active on Twitter at @MissReed where you can engage with her as we continue to impact growth around the world by building community through culturally relevant practices in diversity and inclusion.

The War on Black Boys in Schools: Black Male Educators Can Help

Jason B. Allen

Black male educators are a solution.

Since 2001, I have been advocating and bringing awareness to Black Male Engagement. It was at the University of West Georgia that a group of Black young men and our adviser, Dr. Said Sewell, one of the few Black professors, began an academic mentoring program. Each week we would dress up to change the image of Black males on campus. Then we had study hall because our belief is knowledge is power. Black Male Educators are a solution!

I learned then through our service program in the Carrollton community with local schools the need for mentoring. I encourage Black Male Engagement because Black boys need to have fathers or father figures, grandfathers, uncles, big brothers, etc., reading to them. Black boys having a Black male reading to them is powerful!

> "It's more than just marching through the community with our kids, it's about showing up, being present in the school and reading with them that changes the narrative."
> - Jason B. Allen, EdLanta

Fathers Incorporated is a great example of an organization doing this work. Based in Atlanta, Fathers Incorporated has created a space for Black males to empower Black boys to read. Real Mean Read isn't just an initiative, it's a movement! Black males are the champions Black boys need to succeed. It's partly because we have walked the journey they are currently on; we know how it feels to be a Black boy in America. Saving our boys begins with us. As a Black Male Educator,

I know how critically important it is for Black boys to have Black males engaged in their lives. People ask me what works and I tell them, "Male Engagement!"

Black boys are matriculating through school without the necessary literacy skills needed to be successful as they go on to the next grade level. Black male engagement does increase the interest of reading in Black boys.

I have seen a huge difference in the academic performance of Black boys in schools that have a balanced number of Black Male Educators along with a strong Black Male Engagement Program.

Schools Label Black Boys as Unruly

Schools generally label Black boys as unruly whereas many Black male educators don't! I see so many Black boys who are in trouble or have long discipline records because of poor behaviors and poor choices. Many of the behaviors connect to the social and emotional development of Black boys. Being an "unruly" child in school could have you sent to prison and not just the Principal's office. All parents/guardians raising Black boys should know the definition of an unruly child. It's important because this label is the indicator of how Black boys are placed into the special education, juvenile justice, and/or prison pipelines. As long as I can remember, Black boys have always been highlighted as the poster child for what unruly behavior in American classrooms looks like.

As long as I can remember, Black boys have always been made to be the poster child for what unruly behavior in American classrooms looks like. In fact, from school district discipline reports, we can see how our Black boys have been deemed in crisis due to being the lowest performing academic group yet having disproportionate high rates of high school dropout, suspensions, juvenile justice, and jails. Throughout the history of our Nation, Black boys have been disproportionality thrown into the juvenile justice system. So it is no surprise that the growing number of youths in Georgia's DJJ that is disproportionality affecting Black boys. Discipline write-ups in school really do matter. Student discipline records play a role in the number of Black boys being entered into the juvenile justice system leading to the school to prison pipeline.

Discipline write ups in school really do matter. Student discipline records play a role in the number of Black boys being entered into the juvenile justice system leading to the school to prison pipeline. There needs to be more support for discipline training for students, parents, and educators. The overall lack of support of positive interventions and counseling services in schools negatively impacts the disproportionate number of Black boys in the juvenile justice system. Unruly behavior includes offenses of minors that have legal implications include but are not limited to truancy, running away from home and incorrigibility.

It's important for parents of Black boys to know how the law defines unruly behavior. This helps us change the narrative of how Black boys are unfairly labeled as juvenile delinquents. A juvenile delinquent is defined as one who is charged with an offense which would not be a crime if it were committed by an adult identified as "unruly" behavior. These seven (7) things define the unruly behavior of a juvenile delinquent and how it impacts Black boys in school:

1. Is subject to compulsory school attendance and is habitually and without justification truant from school
2. Is habitually disobedient of the reasonable and lawful commands of the child's parent, guardian, or other custodian and is ungovernable
3. Has committed an offense which is applicable only to a child

4. Has without just cause and without the consent of the child's parent or legal custodian deserted the child's place of abode
5. Wanders or loiters about the streets of any city, or in or about any highway or any public place, between the hours of 12:00 midnight and 5:00 a.m.
6. Disobeys the terms of supervision contained in a court order which has been directed to such child who has been adjudicated unruly
7. Patronizes any bar where alcoholic beverages are being sold, unaccompanied by such child's parent.

> ". . . there are only two options for Black boys in schools; graduation or jail. Black Male Educators can change this!"
> - Jason B. Allen, Educator

Georgia schools provide many options for success to students. If you fall into one of the marginalized groups, your options go from many to few. However, according to one of my former students in presentation almost ten years ago for high school, this isn't the case for Black boys.

Maleek stated in a presentation that there are only two options for Black boys in schools: graduation or jail. This was based on his experience in schools and the lack of Black male teachers. Although ten years later, Maleek's words from that speech still ring out to me. This let me know the urgency in us empowering Black Male Educators that already exist (inside and outside of the classroom) in order to find a place for them in a space that has been uninviting.

> "The underrepresentation of Black Men in the teacher corps not only negatively affects students of color, but all students who enter the classroom." - Fellowship BME

Dr. Danielle Stewart is the founder of the Community Empowerment Foundation, Inc. The mission is to identify issues like this and to educate, advocate and empower US to create the change we want. I've partnered with Dr. Danielle Stewart to bring awareness to mission of The Fellowship of Black Male Educators for Social Justice. Our organizations, In School Spirit and Lillie's Foundation for Change, are joining forces to help bring awareness to the need for more Black Male Educators in schools, Pre-K - higher education, who want to see all students, with a focus on Black boys, thrive and succeed.

Advocating for more Black males to become educators has to be intentional. In speaking with Dr. Stewart, she believes that being intentional in not only the recruitment of Black male educators in the classroom but ALL of our community engagement efforts. "We will help bridge the gap that exists between black males and the culture of educational institutions," she says. To do this, we must first recognize the voice of the Black boys and celebrate their value in our communities and schools. We must also be intentional about training staff who work with Black boys. I've seen faculty and staff members regard Black boys as prisoners.

We must create platforms in our communities that will educate our stakeholders about the true deficit of Black Male Educators in schools. We then must advocate for and with our Black boys who are directly impacted by this problem and embracing their stories as a testimony to answer the *"why"* to this issue.

When we think about the shortage of black male teachers in the classroom, often it is because Black men did not see it themselves or have the experience and exposure to one personally.

Bringing awareness to the need for more Black Male Educators gives the opportunity them the opportunity to teach or lead in multiple roles. This positively impacts the academic settings in schools and give Black boys the opportunities to witness such a rarity.

Black boys should experience having a Black Male Educator throughout their academic career. Through the empowerment of Black Male Engagement, we will improve the options for Black boys in schools.

> "It's appalling and a grave injustice when schools place non-disabled African American students in special education merely on the basis of race."
> - Rev. Augustus Corbett, Esq.

Black boys, often described as unruly in general ed classes, are either placed out temporarily through in-school suspension or are placed in the special education department. Fewer opportunities for gifted programs are afforded to them due to stereotypes of behavior. From my experience, schools don't do enough to encourage or prepare Black boys for rigorous educational programs or opportunities in school. I encourage parents and funders to look at the number of Black boys entering and being retained in gifted and talented programs and honor societies schools offer, and compare that to the numbers of Black boys in special education programs, being assigned in school suspension or being placed out of schools. This shows if school leaders are intentionally planning around the anticipation of the failure of Black boys, not their success. We are always planning and preparing for the failure of Black boys as seen in our Special Education programs and the school to prison pipeline. Be empowered to plan for and embrace their success.

The labeling of Black boys as unruly is one of the major factors to why the numbers of Black boys in special education programs grows. I've witnessed Principals in Charter schools cover up their negligence to meet the needs of students who have IEP's. In fact, they are less likely to hire individuals who can drive academic progress and who are trained in handling "discipline." This is one of the reasons why I support the Dignity in Schools campaign, "Counselors not Cops!" We need more Black Male Educators who can reach and teach Black boys, not cops in schools who treat them like juvenile offenders.

> "We cannot take the silence of Black boys as if they are asleep to the injustice that plagues them. in our schools and our society."
> - Jason B. Allen, Educator

In the last 10 years, I have witnessed Black boys being walked to the path of special education because of who they are, how they behave, and the fear that educators have of them. Stereotypes from the American systems of Black boys will always attribute to the challenges they face in schools.

Our Black boys matriculate through schools with unfinished educational goals and if they aren't pushed out, still leave with unfinished goals. Some of the common obstacles for Black boys in special education programs are:

1. Discipline
2. Lack of engagement
3. Deficiencies in academic fundamentals

Discipline plays a major role in the entry of Black boys in special education. The money is allotted, but the access is not granted for children in special education programs to truly get the services they need to succeed. Our Black boys are shuffled into special education programs, and we don't even have the amount of staff needed or required to service them.

What parents have to manage with one child going through the special education program is like putting three kids through college. The back and forth and lack of support from schools servicing Black boys in special education programs is unbelievable. It's even more challenging when having to deal with a lot of the behaviors Black boys deal with progressing through school. Black Male Educators have a way of connecting with Black boys to inspire and produce academic and social successes.

Black boys don't feel affirmed by being labeled as unruly and pushed in special education programs. In a conversation with my mentees, the boys made a good yet truthful point. Being a Black and being in a special education program in America is being twice marked as less than or abnormal. That is what too many of our Black boys take with them from school. This must change!

About the Author

Jason B. Allen

Over the last 15 years, Jason B. Allen has worked in education servicing our students, families, and communities in various positions from After School Program Director, Teacher Assistant, Associate Teacher, ELA & Reading Teacher (middle and high school), School Parent Liaison, District Family Engagement Specialist and now Dean of School Culture/Assistant Principal. A major goal of his is to ensure that all youth have positive role models to emulate and aspire them to find greatness in their endeavors. Aspiring one day to be a school Principal and build his own school.

Throughout his academic career, he has mentored many young African American males through his national mentoring program, BMWI (Black Men with Initiative), serving as the third National President. He leads his family's foundation, Lillie's Foundation, that supports grandparents raising school-aged children. He has served in various Board Chair capacities, GA Leadership Academy Economic & Leadership Development Certification, 50Can Advocate and GA Forward alumni. He recently finished the Family & Community Engagement Program at Harvard.

Embedding the spirit of service, the main goal of Mr. Allen is to simply help others along his life's journey. He's dedicated to servicing those in need, determined to do the right thing for the right reasons and dependable; living by his word being his bond.

It All Began with Nancy

Amy Storer

It all began with Nancy.

(Original blog posts featured at Converse in the Classroom.)

I can still remember what it felt like to sit in her classroom and watch her with her students. I can still see the colors and hear the music. I can still hear her voice and her laughter. I can still feel what it felt like to belong to a classroom family. It was pure magic. And still today, all these years later, I can feel it in everything I do. It all began with Nancy.

I decided to become an educator because of my mother. For me, there were no other options. I couldn't wait to have a classroom of my own! I started my teaching career in 2005 as a 3rd-grade teacher at the exact same school where my mother had taught and where I attended school.

Had taught. Did you catch that? My mother, my fearless and selfless mother, left her passion. She had to leave to take on a job that paid more, at that time, to help to raise my twin sister and I. Putting two twin girls through college came at a steep price, and as a single mother, she made this decision to best support us. This is another reason why I decided to become an educator. It all began with Nancy.

It was during my first year as a teacher, that my mother was diagnosed with stage 4 ovarian cancer. She was given less than a year to live, and soon after, Hurricane Rita was projected to hit our small town of Fannett, Texas. We quickly evacuated and headed north to escape this violent storm. While we were evacuated, we secured my mother an appointment at MD Anderson in Houston, Texas. They were our butterflies in the storm. They gave my mother hope.

One of my favorite quotes by Helen Keller is, "Optimism is the faith that leads to achievement. Nothing can be done without hope and confidence." My mother had hope and confidence, and she set a goal. She was going to teach again. It all began for Nancy.

During my second year as an educator, my mother was hired to teach first grade at the very same school that I was teaching. It was a dream come true! Not only was my mother reunited with her passion, but she was going to teach with me. With me! I had dreamed about this since I first decided to become a teacher. But life had other plans for us. Shortly into the school year, my mother became very ill, and it was soon discovered that the cancer had returned. My mother, Nancy, passed away in October of 2006. I will forever treasure the small amount of time that I had to teach with my mother. I will treasure every pass in the hallway, every visit in the lunchroom, and each time she just stopped by to say hi. How lucky was I to get this time with her while we were both doing what we loved...educating and loving our students. It was pure magic.

I truly believed that the hole in my heart would never repair. And I was content with that. Life showed me that I was wrong in the most beautiful way possible. My niece, Nancy Ann Langham, was born in September of 2011. My heart began to beat again. She breathed life back into me, and that hole that I was positive would never fill back up, was now completely filled in. It all began with Nancy.

Nancy is now 7 years old, and she reminds me so much of my mother. Much like my mother motivated and influenced my educational footprints, even after she was gone, Nancy now does the same. Almost every move I make as an educator is because of that small soul or for her. There is a reason why I shared this part of my life with you. I wanted to take you back to where it all started to show you and make you fully understand the journey that has led me to this chapter. It all began with Nancy.

Not too long ago, I was sitting next to Nancy, and I told her that I loved her. As soon as I said it, I asked myself, "Am I telling her this enough?" Do I tell her that she is strong and beautiful and everything in between? Have I told her that she is the half to my whole heart? That she is the vivid color in the dark? That I can't wait to see where her life takes her? To answer that first question, what is enough? There shouldn't be a cap on how many times you say I love you or how many times you show the ones you love how much you care.

I often wonder if our kids, our students, are hearing these things as much as they should in our classrooms or as much as they deserve. Are they hearing that they will move mountains with every word spoken? That they will rattle and shake the norms of society? That they are loved and appreciated for being exactly who they were meant to be?

Love them. When they fight and struggle, love them. When they tell you they don't care, love them. When they turn away, love them, and remind them of that daily. Love them on good days and bad. Love them all. You might be the only bright light that they've seen in a while. Make sure your time with them is intentional and full of love and laughter. Just love them. We all make a choice as educators on how we choose to impact the life of a child. Our job is such an important one.

Teach as if it is your last day on Earth. Teach as if it is the last time that you will have the chance to change a child's life. Teach for whomever your "Nancy" is in your life.

It all began with...

About the Author

Amy Storer

    Amy is a graduate of Lamar University with a Master's in Educational Technology Leadership. She truly loves being an instructional coach for Montgomery ISD. This is her 3rd year as a campus coach, and she is so happy to be at their newest elementary school, Keenan Elementary. She has taught grades 1-4, and she is also a technology integration mentor for her district. She holds two

Teacher of the Year distinctions and, in 2015, was a top 4 finalist in HEB's Excellence in Education in the "Leadership Elementary" category. Amy is an educator that encourages and motivates others to reach far beyond the classroom walls to make the learning more meaningful and inspiring. She has a true passion for working with other educators and students to encourage them to make and foster global connections.

Ever-Changing Nature & Needs

Dene Gainey

The one thing in life that we can guarantee is change.

One of the greatest realizations an educator might have is the need to not settle into a place. The word *place* could be geographical or metaphorical. It has been said many times that the only constant in life is change. How do we [educators] remain the same when the students we serve change each year, both naturally as well as their needs?

While often there are often expectations of classroom teachers that limit the flexibility they have, the benefits of focusing on the students as part of a wider desire to meet the needs of all learners is a greater focus.

What do Students Need?

In a study by Uslu and Gizir (2016), it was observed that among other variables, "teacher-student relationships are the most important predictive variable of adolescents' sense of school belonging" (p. 74). As the phrase goes, "students don't care how much you know until they know how much you care." I've always believed an educator's role far superseded a focus on academics. Needs are specific to the student, and on any given day, that could mean a number of different things.

In a recent conversation with students, I addressed the need for more than academics. Developing academic success is awesome and a necessary component on this journey of progression into responsible, dutiful individuals. However, I admonished the students saying that academics are but only a piece of the puzzle. There is also a need to develop good character.

Maslow's work provides a great foundation for physiological needs (Aruma & Hanachor, 2017). Bloom also brings academic needs to the table (Forehand, 2005). Perhaps we have all heard the phrase, "Maslow before Blooms." There is great truth in this natural progression of things. If I don't have my physiological needs met, then I may not produce much when approached by a teacher who wants me to learn academically. That is not to say I won't learn, but my focus may not be completely on learning when I am worried about how I will eat when I get home.

Once Maslow is accomplished, then, by all means, let us get into Bloom's. "Teaching is certainly about more than curriculum; teachers can use instructional technologies to develop learning experiences that prepare students for effective citizenship" (Frye, Trathen & Koppenhaver, 2010). It's easy to understand that technology refers to the electronic devices that are a huge hit with children.

What may not be as clear is that according to the Collins English dictionary (n.d.), the definition of technology is the *methods, systems, and devices which are the result of scientific knowledge being used for practical purposes.* This definition suggests that more than electronics, technology is broad and includes more than just "devices."

The Need to Change

Teaching is a reflexive process. If I taught every day and never evaluated the influence or impact of teaching, I'd never know whether the strategies, tools, and actions executed are effective. If I don't reflect, I may limit my capacity for growth. Reflection includes critique, review and sets the stage for improvement. Reflection empowers me to see what worked but also challenges me to explore new areas of interest concerning the most important stakeholder. One of the best things an educator can do is to change.

I joined Twitter in May of 2015 and have never looked back. Many opportunities for learning and engagement have arisen from my Twitter activity. I have been challenged, encouraged and motivated to *be different, be authentic, and be relevant.* The days change, the needs change, the time changes, the resources change, students change, and therefore I feel the need to change too. Sometimes that means embracing the newness of teaching and learning. What's new? What's hot? What's not? How can I be the best version of me in the classroom so that I can deliver the best content possible and empower and reach my students in the way(s) in which they need to be reached? *It is not just about the teach, but it is about the reach.*

The Need to Reach

I think back to my childhood, not too long ago. I remember being very attentive and willing to learn in ways that were presented to me at the time. Some aspects of technology were not available. I didn't have a cell phone until I went to high school and it started out as a fat, heavy electronic device that would not even function today.

I had skilled and dedicated teachers who were willing to do what it took to help me. This included letting me help them (partly the reason I teach today) and dedicating time to me after school and during lunch to ensure I gained knowledge of content. While some were at times abrasive, they meant well, and I am here today thanks to the efforts of my teachers.

When I started teaching, I was excited, motivated, and ready for adventure. I believed that learning should be fun, and I tried my hardest in every task to ensure that happened. In fact, I still have a desire to innovate, immerse, and engage students in the learning process. One thing I realize, though, is the change that has taken place in me over the twelve years I've been in the classroom. I've noticed some massive changes as well as some seemingly small things too.

A small (yet big) change is the move towards a hybrid blended learning environment. Paper is great and still has its purpose, but with technology promoting access, feedback and motivation, the use of technology as integrated into the curriculum has been nothing but positive. Now using an electronic platform called "[Fresh Grade]()," I am able to embed learning, as well as provide constant ongoing feedback in a space where learning is authentic to the student. This is a great example of reach.

Students love texting, as well as taking video, pictures, and audio of themselves. Moreover, students love being able to demonstrate their learning in meaningful ways—ways that mean something to them.

How do you reach students today? Is the reach today the same as the reach twelve years ago? Absolutely not! I'm sure there are many variables to consider why it may take more today or an alternative approach today. What we can conclude is that it makes us better and more versatile educators when our goal is to reach and not just teach.

I would not be able to do what I do today without the constant doors and hallways of learning. I would not be relevant today had it not been for the desire to reach students. Yes, I want to change their years, but moreover, I want to change their lives.

Broadening the Level of Impact

So how do you broaden the impact? I believe it is first a change of mind. We should not limit our capacities to make a difference. Sometimes it's that one thing you do that creates a domino effect. It's that one time you listened to a child's thoughts, and as a result, they felt empowered to "BE." I have enjoyed being able to create activities, even alongside students whereby their interest is increased because of their participation in its development.

I love Inquiry-Based Learning as it challenges students to ask relevant questions that might lead to developing potential solutions. Not only that, it provides an opportunity for the teacher to help students make connections between the curriculum and society, making it meaningful to their lives. I think it is also a great opportunity to participate in learning with students.

Project-Based Learning is always fun because it lets students shine. Students get to show off their thinking, their process(es), their product(s), connections made and synthesis. I love the variety and authenticity embedded within project-based learning because no two products are the same. More than the product though, it is intriguing to watch and listen to the process, specifically the level of growth, including language development, reasoning, and decision-making.

I love Problem-Based Learning and Challenge-Based Learning because students get to branch out of the four walls of the classroom and live in the world, immersing themselves in the various challenges that individuals face. It allows the human part of us to come out, not to mention the empathy and opportunity for growth, empowerment, and change in us all.

What I know to be true is that our one constant in life is change. Things will not stay the same. The weather in Florida will be warm at some point, but there is a guarantee of some change from day-to-day or even hour-to-hour. It is change in the earth's position relative to the sun that causes Earth to experience seasons. It is our location on the earth that determines whether we are experiencing day or night, as the world turns. Change is all around us. Let's be the change we want to see in our classrooms.

References

Aruma, E. & Hanachor, M. (2017). Abraham Maslow's hierarchy of needs and assessment of needs in community development. International Journal of Development and Economic Sustainability 5(7), pp.15-27

Collins Dictionary. (n.d.). Definition of 'technology.' Retrieved November 24, 2018, from https://www.collinsdictionary.com/us/dictionary/english/technology

Forehand, M. (2005). Bloom's taxonomy. Retrieved from: https://www.d41.org/cms/lib/IL01904672/Centricity/Domain/422/BloomsTaxonomy.pdf

Frye, E. M., Trathen, W., & Koppenhaver, D. A. (2010). Internet workshop and blog publishing: Meeting student (and teacher) learning needs to achieve best practice in the twenty-first-century social studies classroom. *Social Studies, 101*(2), 46–53. https://doi-org.lopes.idm.oclc.org/10.1080/00377990903284070

Uslu, F., & Gizir, S. (n.d.). School belonging of adolescents: The role of teacher-student relationships, peer relationships and family involvement. *Educational Sciences-Theory & Practice, 17*(1), 63–82. https://doi-org.lopes.idm.oclc.org/10.12738/estp.2017.1.0104

About the Author

Dene Gainey

Dene Gainey is an educator and lifelong learner from Orlando, FL with a Bachelor of Science in Elementary Education and a Master's of Education in Instructional Technology, and is a current doctoral student. Currently with twelve years of teaching experience, Dene functions in various capacities in the education world to include teaching

English-Language Arts, technology gifted students.

Dene has a passion for the C.L.I.M.B.E., celebrating diversity, building community, project-based and problem-based learning as well as the student-driven classroom. As an educator, Dene feels it is his niche to build bridges and fill gaps, not to mention to give meaning to learning experiences and use all of his skills and talents as a means to motivate students to be "more." As a veteran of the United States Air Force, a singer and songwriter, actor and author collectively, Dene incorporates techniques in the classroom to cultivate an environment where learning happens in various ways.

He recently collaborated in the EduSnap 2016 "Best Practices in Education" publication, with his chapter called "The Student-Driven Classroom." He also is a contributing author for the EduSnap 2017 edition with a chapter titled "Celebrating Diversity & Building Community." His "one word" that encapsulates his day-to-day role and function in the classroom is "IMPACT."

EduMatch Snapshot in Education (2018)

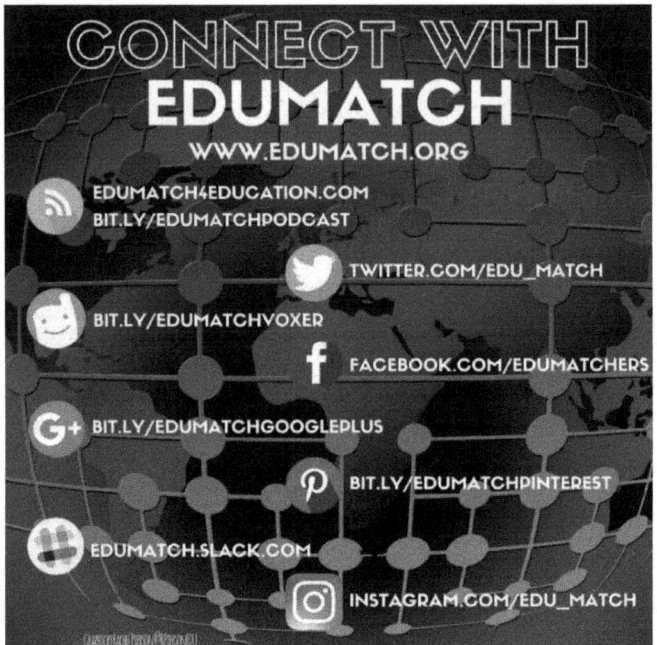

Visit us at edumatch.org

Coming Soon: Snapshot in Education 2019

Now seeking interested authors. Please inquire at:

books.edumatch.org/edusnapinterestform.

Other EduMatch Books

In this collaborative project, twenty educators located throughout the United States share educational strategies that have worked well for them, both with students and in their professional practice.

Hey there, awesome educator! We know how busy you are. Trust us, we get it. Dive in as fourteen international educators share their recipes for success, both literally and metaphorically! In this book, we come together to support one another not only in the classroom, but also in the kitchen.

We're back! EduMatch proudly presents Snapshot in Education (2017). In this two-volume collection, 32 educators and one student share their tips for the classroom and professional practice. Topics include culture, standards, PBL, instructional models, perseverance, equity, PLN, and more.

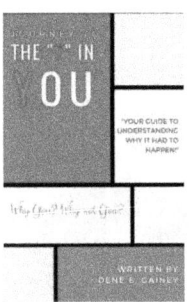

This book started as a series of separate writing pieces that were eventually woven together to form a fabric called The Y in You. The question is, "What's the 'why' in you?" Why do you? Why would you? Why should you? Through the pages in this book, you will gain the confidence to be you, and understand the very power in what being you can produce.

Follow the Teacher's Journey with Brian as he weaves together the stories of seven incredible educators. Each step encourages educators at any level to reflect, grow, and connect. The Teacher's Journey will ignite your mind and heart through its practical ideas and vulnerable storytelling.

Adversity itself is not what defines us. It is how we react to that adversity and the choices we make that creates who we are and how we will persevere. The Fire Within: Lessons from defeat that have ignited a passion for learning is a compilation of stories from amazing educators who have faced personal adversity head on and have become stronger people for it. They use their new-found strength to support the students and teachers they work with.

This book challenges the thought that "teaching" begins only after certification and college graduation. Instead, it describes how students in teacher preparation programs have value to offer their future colleagues, even as they are learning to be teachers! This book provides positive examples, helpful tools, and plenty of encouragement for preservice teachers to learn, to dream, and to do.

The maker mindset sets the stage for the Fourth Industrial Revolution, empowering educators to guide their students to pursue a path of learning that is meaningful to them. Addressing a shifting culture in today's classrooms, we look to scaling up and infusing this vision in a classroom, in a school, and even in a district.

The concept of being innovative can be made to sound so simple. We think of a new idea. We take a risk and implement the new idea. We fail, learn, and move forward. But what if the development of the innovative thinking isn't the only roadblock? What if so much of your day is spent solving the issues around you that even the attempt at developing new ideas is not even on your radar? What if you long to have more divergent teachers in your school district or to be that divergent teacher, but you simply don't know where to start?

www.ingramcontent.com/pod-product-compliance
Lightning Source LLC
Chambersburg PA
CBHW070546050426
42450CB00011B/2741